Twilight of the Gods

TWILIGHT

OF THE

GODS

The Mayan Calendar and the Return of the Extraterrestrials

Erich
von Däniken

Translated by Nicholas Quaintmere

Foreword by Giorgio Tsoukalos

New Page Books
A division of The Career Press, Inc.
Pompton Plains, NJ

TWILIGHT OF THE GODS

EDITED BY JODI BRANDON

TYPESET BY EILEEN MUNSON

Cover design by Howard Grossman/12E Designs
Printed in the U.S.A. by Courier

To order this title, please call toll-free 1-800-CAREER-1 (NJ and Canada: 201-848-0310) to order using VISA or MasterCard, or for further information on books from Career Press.

The Career Press, Inc., 220 West Parkway, Unit 12
Pompton Plains, NJ 07417
www.careerpress.com
www.newpagebooks.com

Library of Congress Cataloging-in-Publication Data

Däniken, Erich von, 1935-

[Götterdämmerung. English]

Twilight of the gods : the Mayan calendar and the return of the extraterrestrials / by Erich von Däniken ; foreword by Giorgio Tsoukalos.

p. cm.

Includes bibliographical references and index.

ISBN 978-1-60163-141-1 – ISBN 978-1-60163-686-7 (ebook) 1. Maya calendar. 2. Two thousand twelve, A.D. 3. Mayas--Folklore. 4. Gods. 5. Extraterrestrial beings. 6. Civilization--Extraterrestrial influences. 7. Tiahuanacu (Bolivia) I. Title.

F1435.3.C14D36 2010

984'.12--dc22

2010018964

Contents

FOREWORD

What is a "cargo cult"? The term refers to the real-life ethnological phenomenon of what happens when a *technologically* primitive society comes in contact with a *technologically* more advanced society. On countless documented occasions, ethnologists have observed that if *technologically advanced visitors live among technologically—not intellectually!*—primitive cultures for short periods of time and then leave, soon thereafter, the visitors' advanced nuts-and-bolts technologies cause the native population to view these rather ordinary humans as gods and begin to worship them. On many occasions during their stay, the visitors would interact with the native population, giving them goods and food—*cargo*! After the departure of these "gods," the native culture surmised that they would return if they practiced intense worship, sacrifice, and emulation. Examples of modern-day cargo cult behavior can be found in the regions of the South Pacific during WWII. Why is this phenomenon so important?

It is important because if cargo cult behavior still takes place today, then it is a rather logical conclusion that cargo cult behavior also took place thousands and thousands of years ago. The cargo cult phenomenon illustrates the basic premise of the classic Ancient Astronaut Theory: Thousands and thousands of years ago, technologically advanced *flesh and blood* extraterrestrials arrived on Earth in *nuts-and-bolts* spaceships. *Intellectually* speaking, our ancestors were *not* stupid (they essentially had the same brain as we have today); however, because their *technological* frame of reference was limited, they did not comprehend the nuts-and-bolts aspects behind the arrival of those flesh and blood extraterrestrials, and so our ancestors *misinterpreted* them as being divine in nature, which, of course, the visitors were *not*. And thus, the "gods" were born. Out of a simple (yet major!) *misunderstanding*.

According to the ancient texts and traditions, a long, long time ago, the gods (lowercase "g") descended from the sky and instructed mankind in various disciplines. Why is it so hard for us to believe, living in a culture so rich in metaphor, that our ancestors drew similar comparisons? Is it *really* such a stretch of the imagination that whatever is described in the ancient texts is nothing more than the description of misunderstood, flesh and blood extraterrestrials who arrived here in nuts-and-bolts spaceships?

Mainstream science believes it is. They believe that *all* of these ancient stories and traditions are a figment of our ancestors' imagination and that all of those legends were nothing but fantasy. But can something *really* be created out of thin air?

For many years, I attended an international boarding school high up in the mountains of Switzerland. After the breakup of the Soviet Union, our school welcomed a few new students from the former USSR. I remember sitting in art class, and our assignment for the day was to draw a "fantasy castle," a "dream castle" floating in the clouds with shining towers and magnificent architectural features. The assigned project sent the entire classroom into a tizzy and we started drawing with unbridled enthusiasm. Everyone, that is, except our three new Russian classmates. None of them touched their pencils. They just sat in front of their large, empty sheets of paper. "What's wrong?" the teacher asked. "Why aren't you drawing?" The students replied: "What's a fantasy castle? What does it look like? We've never seen one. Since we've never seen one, we can't draw it." What an extraordinary reaction!

This incident underscores one point: If something has not been *seen,* then it *cannot* be invented. Translation: It is *impossible* to conjure up something out of thin air if the *basic elements* are missing. *Nothing happens without the initial spark of inspiration, without a catalyst.* Therefore, mythologies, legends, tales, *whatever*—which mainstream science today discredits as mere fantasy inventions of our ancestors' imagination—*cannot* possibly *all* be unfounded inventions or mere fig-ments of someone's imagination. Quite on the contrary! *Something* had to be there in the first place to act as the catalyst, the basic element that sparked the story. *Something* happened to our ancestors; they witnessed something that compelled them to tell of these events in their traditions.

I think we'd all have to agree that it is *impossible* to create, let alone solve, an algebraic equation *without* knowing the basics of mathematics. It *cannot* be done. In this scenario, the basic mathematical elements represent the aforementioned initial spark, the catalyst. Everything else follows quite naturally *afterward.*

It is said that each legend has a true core. It is this core that repre-sents the base element, the catalyst. Without a base element, or initial inspiration, nothing is possible. Therefore, if something like this hap-pened to my Russian classmates living in the 20th century, then why couldn't something similar have happened to our ancestors many thou-sands of years ago? The Ancient Astronaut Theory shows that it has.

We must remind ourselves that when all of these legends and stories first were written down, the art of writing itself was a fairly new inven-tion. Our ancestors realized very quickly that this new invention was the most powerful tool with which to preserve important knowledge. Is it re-ally logical to think that the first stories and legends put in writing by our ancestors were only figments of their imagination? Of course not! Why?

Our ancestors lived in a time fraught with uncertainty and upheav-al. The most important order of the day was raw survival, the gathering of food, finding of shelter. So it is a logical conclusion that the first people empowered with the written word had *better* things to do than to sit around a fire, get drunk, and invent fantasy stories! "What story shall we conjure up tonight so we can painstakingly carve this stuff into stone?" But that is *exactly* what mainstream science proposes: *All* an-cient stories are made up so that the story-tellers could "come to grips" with the world and its surroundings. I consider this type of thinking to be an insult to the intelligence of our ancestors.

I hear the Ancient Astronaut Theory is insulting to our ancestors because it "undermines human ingenuity." I ask you, *who exactly* is insulting our ancestors' intelligence and ingenuity by pompously insisting that the records of our ancestors are "false" or that "they made mistakes in recording some dates" etc.? It is most certainly *not* the Ancient Astronaut Theory.

With the invention of the written word, *for the first time in human history,* people were able to permanently record the most significant events of *their time.* Just like we have newspapers and books today, in which we report about things that are important to us, why would it have been any different for our ancestors?

For example, Native Americans still today refer to a train as a "fire horse," a throwback to a time when they did not have the word "train" in their vocabulary. The same applies to the things and events our ancestors wrote down. They had no way of calling a flying object by the words "aircraft" or "plane," so they did the next best thing: They *described* it with objects with which they were most familiar in their everyday lives. *Misunderstood technology.* So if there are detailed, intricate descriptions of beings that descended from the sky on flying shields or fiery chariots and taught ancient humanity in various academic disciplines in the remote past, then we must start to explore these accounts from another perspective.

What they immortalized at the time was *their history! Their lives!* They diligently recorded and attempted to *circumscribe* events that *really* happened to them (or *their* ancestors). Little did they know that future "scientists" would relegate their writings into the realm of symbolism and fantasy. *That* type of pompous attitude shows a great disrespect to our ancestors, *not* the idea that extraterrestrials showed up here on Earth thousands of years ago.

Five hundred years from now, after establishing permanent bases on the Moon and Mars, humanity will venture out to explore deep space. One of our generation spaceships will eventually arrive at a planet harboring intelligent life. What if the intelligent life we encounter turns out to be *technologically* primitive? What will we do? Will we just stand back and study them from afar? Yes, maybe for a month or two. But then, after we have studied and mastered their language (as ethnologists do every day), we *will* make *physical* contact with them because, well, that's what we do—we poke and prod at things because we can't help ourselves. We *will* interfere with their cultural development. We *will* guide their technological direction. We *will* give them a gentle push. We *will* teach them a few things. We *will* make them aware of the essentials of science and various academic disciplines.

And many, many generations *after* our departure, our "ancient" visit *will* be regarded as myth and fantasy because accounts of our visit in ancient texts will be deemed as "unscientific" by the oh-so-smart scientists of that society ("A long time ago, the gods descended from the sky and taught our forefathers! etc."). By now that society will also have reached such an "advanced" technological development that it now readies itself to go into deep space. But *our* physical visit *will* be regarded as a figment of *their* ancestors' imagination and relegated into the realm of quirky mythology because it is "preposterous" to read ancient history as recordings of actual events. Remind you of anyone? *And thus the cycle begins anew....*

One day in the not-too-distant future, we, too, *will* become Ancient Astronauts ourselves on some faraway planet. So why couldn't this have happened here on Earth, thousands and thousands of years ago? The answer is self-evident, and it's time we shed our arrogant attitude and opened our minds to what *really* happened in our cosmic past.

With my very best regards,

Giorgio A. Tsoukalos

Director, Center for Ancient Astronaut Research/A.A.S. R.A.

Publisher, *Legendary Times Magazine*

PREFACE

So, how did it all begin?

Let's turn the clock back around 65 years. We find ourselves in a primary school in the town of Schaffhausen, Switzerland. And there I am! I'm 10 years old and listening to my religious education teacher describe a battle that took place up in heaven. And here's how it went: One day, the archangel Lucifer and his heavenly host marched up to the throne of God and declared: "We will serve you no longer!" Thereupon the Almighty God ordered his archangel Michael to expel Lucifer and his entire gang of hangers on out of heaven forever. Since then—my teacher explained—Lucifer has been the Devil, and all of his followers have roasted in the infernal fires of hell.

Well, this certainly gave me something to ponder about, and that evening, perhaps for the first time in my life, I sat down and did some really serious thinking. Heaven, we had always been told, was a place of absolute bliss, a sanctuary where all good people would head off to after shuffling off this mortal coil. It was also the place where all souls would spend eternity in heavenly unity with God. So how could a quarrel like this come about in paradise, where all is bathed in divine happiness and where perfect unity with God abounds? Surely, discord would be completely impossible in a place like that, wouldn't it? Why should Lucifer and his angels suddenly take up arms against the almighty and benevolent God?

I went to my mother and asked her advice, but she couldn't come up with a satisfactory response either. In God's realm, she said, groping for some kind of answer, everything is possible. And that seems to be it: Everything is possible—even the impossible.

When I was 16, I was sent to a boarding school run by Jesuits. We learned Latin and Greek, and I realized that the word *Lucifer* derived from two words: *lux* (light) and *ferre* (bear, carry). So Lucifer actually means bringer or bearer of light. The Devil, of all people, the bringer of light? My new knowledge of Latin just made the matter all the more confusing.

Ten years later I had studied the Old Testament, as Christians call the ancient text, in great depth. This is what I read in the Book of the Prophet Isaiah (from around 740 BC):

> "O how you have fallen from Heaven, O morning star, son of the dawn! How you have fallen to Earth, and laid the nations low! For you said in your heart, I will go up to heaven, will make my seat higher than the stars of God; I will take my place on the mountain of the meeting-place of the gods..." (Isaiah 14:12–13).

Most likely, the sayings of the Prophet Isaiah have changed somewhat over the millennia. So what was their original meaning? If you look a little further, you'll find another clear reference to war in paradise:

> "And there was war in Heaven: Michael and his angels went out to the fight with the dragon. And the dragon and his angels made war. And they were overcome, and there was no more place for them in heaven." (Revelation 12:7).

Battles *in heaven*? In space perhaps? Were our unknowing forefathers simply trying to express the inner struggle between good and evil that takes place in all of us? Did they misinterpret the atmospheric battle that rages during a thunder storm as a war in the heavens? The dark clouds against the sun? Or was the root of their confusion a solar eclipse, where it seemed that something monstrous was devouring the sun? All of these naturalistic explanations, however, don't quite cut the mustard, as I later realized after comparing these writings with ancient texts from other cultures.

Greek mythology, for instance, also begins with a heavenly battle. According to the Greeks, the children of Ouranos rejected heavenly order and their creator. This led to terrible bloodshed—and Zeus, the father of the gods, was just one of the victors.

All the way over on the other side of the world—and a long way away from Greece!—lies New Zealand. Its original residents, the Maori, have legends that also begin with a heavenly war. Again, a group of the gods' children rebelled against their fathers. The leader of those heavenly warriors was called Rongamai, and after his victory he settled with his people on the Earth.

You can imagine how my sensitive young psyche was thrown into confusion as I was given the task of translating Chapter 19, Verse 12 ff. of Exodus from the Old Testament. I read how the "Lord" descended to a mountain in Exodus, Chapter 19, Verse 18 ff: "Mount Sinai was swathed in smoke, because the LORD had come down on it in fire. And the smoke ascended like the smoke from a furnace, and the whole mount quaked greatly."

Let me make one thing clear: I have always believed in God, and I still pray regularly. But *my* dear God has to have certain qualities. He is timeless—in other words, he doesn't need to do experiments and wait to see how they turn out. He knows already. He is almighty and omnipresent. He doesn't need any kind of vehicle to move from point A to B. Why should God need some kind of flaming carriage to descend onto a mountain and reduce everything to fire and smoke—so much so that the mountain shakes? The very mountain that Moses was required to fence off for safety reasons. What on earth is being described here?

Later I read the experiences of the Prophet Ezekiel in the Bible. He also described a vehicle with wings, wheels, and metal legs and that caused an awful noise and threw sand up into the air. The Lord's chariot-throne? My dear God doesn't ride around in that kind of vehicle! To be honest, I find it insulting to the omnipresent God to maintain that he would be so insignificant that he would need to use any kind of transport at all!

Suddenly, I was plagued with doubts about my own religion. As a young man, I wanted to know if other ancient peoples told the same kind of strange stories as the Israelites in the Bible. And that's where it all started. I got stuck in and began researching. Thus began a fascinating life that has been filled with ups and downs and has taken me halfway across the world. It has led me to visit the world's greatest libraries. It has caused me to seek out and talk to many highly educated and intelligent people. It has moved me to visit countless archaeological excavations. And, last but not least, it inspired me to start writing. I wrote my very first book, *Chariots of the Gods,* at the tender age of 33, while I was still working full time as the director of a top-class hotel.

Twilight of the Gods is my 25th nonfiction book! Add to that my collaborations on seven anthologies and—just on the side—the six novels I've written, and you've got quite a collection. I've had a bit of fun recently counting up all the nonfiction pages I've published: 8,342 pages! Looks like a number you might see on a check.

Eight thousand, three hundred forty-two pages! Would you believe it? Doesn't the guy ever run out of things to say? Surely, he must repeat himself quite a lot!

To be honest, the reason that it never gets boring is because the material just keeps coming and coming! The field I work in never stops getting more exciting and more up-to-date. Increasing numbers of authors and scientists are becoming fascinated by the subject. And that's not really any great surprise. After all, the thought that extraterrestrials were here thousands of years ago is one that touches on a whole range of different scientific fields. So what are we talking about? Well, it involves prehistory, archeology, philology (especially linguistics), ethnology, evolution, genetics, philosophy, astronomy, astrophysics, exobiology, space travel, and, of course, one mustn't forget theology.

Repetitions? Well, they're impossible to avoid completely. For instance, I already dedicated 12 pages in my book *The Stones of Kiribati* to the enigmatic ruins in Puma Punku in the highlands of Bolivia, and now I've come back to the subject. Why, you ask?

Well, it's like this: In the past, I dealt with Puma Punku more like a journalist. I reported on it and presented a number of pictures without ever really going into any depth on the subject. But this time, I'd like to document what it was that left the very first visitors breathless and stammering as they stood before the mighty stone blocks of Puma Punku 400 years ago. I'd like to show you what archaeologists discovered hundreds of years ago and demonstrate how much has been destroyed throughout the centuries. Intentionally. But I will also prove that Puma Punku was not built by any Stone Age people.

And in December 2012, the gods will return from their long journey and appear again here on Earth. At least that is what the Mayan calendar, and Mayan written and oral lore, would have us believe. This time, I've gone into greater depth than ever before. The so-called gods—in other words, the extraterrestrials—will come again. We're in store for a "god shock" of major proportions.

Doesn't anyone with half a brain know that interstellar travel is simply impossible and is likely to remain so because of the huge distances between the stars? And that extraterrestrials would never look like us?

Well, my dear readers, I destroy these preconceptions. Systematically. One little piece at a time. I hope you enjoy reading about it!

Yours,

Erich von Däniken
September 2009

CHAPTER 1

A BASE CAMP FOR THE GODS

What would you say if I told you there is a place 13,000 feet high up in the Andes that, according to ancient Inca traditions, was built in a single night by the gods? A place where huge stone slabs lie strewn around like discarded playing cards on the floor? Stone slabs that have been carefully cut and transported and yet about which the Spanish chroniclers—writing 400 years ago—said that no man could have moved? A place where gigantic blocks of andesite were cut and worked with incredible precision and archeologists expect us to believe that it was Stone Age men that did it? A place in which a calendar was discovered that reaches back 15,000 years into the past? A calendar that even shows the phases of the moon for every day and every hour!

Let me tell you: This place really exists. It's called Tiwanaku, and it lies high in the Bolivian Andes. So why have we never heard of this place? Why hasn't *National Geographic* or the Discovery Channel produced groundbreaking documentaries about it? Is there some sort of conspiracy going on? Or has this sensational discovery simply gone up in a puff of smoke?

One of the reasons for this deafening silence is a friend of Adolf Hitler and well-known antisemite named Hans Hörbiger, an eccentric of the kind that only recognizes one truth—his own. People like this are never written about—even when they occasionally come up with extremely valid points. So just who was this guy?

Hans Hörbiger was born in 1860 to a well-to-do family in the Tyrol region. He studied engineering at the Technical University in Vienna and after graduating worked initially as a technical draftsman at a factory building steam engines. Eventually he transferred to the Land Company, where he worked as a compressor specialist. In

1894, he devised a new valve system for pumps and compressors. He patented his new invention and licensed it to a number of German and foreign firms. For a while it made him quite a rich man, but much of his fortune was wiped out—first by the hyperinflation of the Twenties and subsequently the Second World War.

As a young engineer, Hörbiger one day observed molten steel flowing over a blanket of snow. It struck him how the snow and earth veritably exploded due to the heat of the steel. It gave him a quite interesting idea: What if the same process were taking place in a kind of eternal struggle throughout the entire universe? Ice and fire—life and death. Hörbiger postulated that throughout the cosmos, huge heavenly bodies would be constantly colliding with mighty chunks of ice and consequently exploding. The resulting debris would form planets and moons. This was the basis of the "World Ice Theory" that Hans Hörbiger published in 1913.

According to this World Ice Theory, our Earth has harbored numerous highly developed cultures that existed in various geological ages—before today's moon even came into existence. These cultures were always destroyed when mighty boulders approached from space and exploded in our atmosphere. The debris that thundered down onto the Earth has caused such catastrophes as the Flood and the downfall of Atlantis. In Hörbiger's opinion, mankind was already highly civilized in the tertiary era. The moon that arose during the tertiary crashed down to Earth, according to Hörbiger, 25,000 years ago, causing all of the lands in the tropics to flood—with the exception of a few high peaks in the Andes and Ethiopia.

Hans Hörbiger was a wrathful prophet indeed! And he certainly had the look for it: He wore his white beard long, and had a permanently fierce expression. On top of that, he had handwriting that was virtually unreadable. Rather egocentrically, he viewed himself as one of the world's great scholars and the *only* one who proclaimed the truth. Accordingly, he demanded radical recognition from the scientific community of the mid-1920s. His way of thinking was much like Hitler's—and vice versa. In his unholy zeal, Hörbiger tolerated no opposition, damning the mathematical and astrophysical knowledge of the times as worthless lies.

Hitler and Hörbiger

In the scientific and technology-fixated world of pre-war Germany, Hans Hörbiger blazed his trail with a mixture of dogmatism, brute force, and alleged enlightenment. Together with his students, he began agitating among the circles of the intelligentsia. Lacking any sort of scruples and utterly immune to criticism, he invested some of his not-insubstantial wealth to set up a movement that was made up of paying members and also had its own small elite troop unit. Adherents plastered the walls of universities and sports stadiums with posters, and handbills were distributed by the thousand. Lectures held by astronomers who disagreed with Hörbiger's opinions were disrupted with boos and ironic laughter, and professors were badgered on the streets. Hörbiger wrote to well-known engineers and astronomers: "Either you must learn to believe in me, or I must treat you as my enemy."[1]

The Hörbiger movement published a total of three extensive reference works and 40 further books aimed at a wider audience. Not only that, there were countless pamphlets and brochures. Their monthly magazine, *Der Schlüssel zum Weltgeschehen* (*The Key to World Events*), achieved a circulation of 100,000 copies.

Hitler believed in Hörbiger and supported him publicly. They also met many times. Hitler listened avidly to Hörbiger's lectures, even though the irascible Hörbiger wouldn't allow even the Führer to interrupt. In one of the pamphlets the group published at the time, one can read: "One Austrian, Hitler, banished the Jewish politicians. A second Austrian, Hörbiger, will banish the Jewish scientists too!"[2]

Luis Pauwels and Jacques Bergier, two great French thinkers and journalists, wrote about Hörbiger's teachings:

> Hörbiger claims that he can reveal the truths about our planet's earliest history as well as its distant future. He throws all current theories on the history of cultures, the appearance and development of mankind and his societies simply out of the window. Hundreds of thousands, if not millions, of years ago, he maintains, there already existed god-like peoples, giants and highly developed cultures...the entire universe is undergoing a kind of uniform phase of development; it is a living organism in which every part exerts an influence on every other part. The quest of mankind is linked to the quest of the stars; everything that happens in the cosmos is reflected in events on the Earth, and vice versa.[3]

But what has all this got to do with the highlands of Bolivia and mysterious ruined city of Tiwanaku?

1.1. The Gateway of the Sun in Tiwanaku. Image courtesy of Tatjana Ingold, Solothurn, Switzerland.

The answer is that one of Hörbiger's followers was an archaeologist, a certain Dr. Edmund Kiss, who spent nine years carrying out research in the highlands of the Andes. There, in Tiwanaku, a monolithic gateway had been discovered—what is today known as the "Gateway of the Sun." For Edmund Kiss, the engravings on this sun gate represented some kind of calendar. It was possible, he claimed, to read the solstices, the equinoxes, every day of the year, the position of the moon for every hour—and all of this data even took into account the rotation of the Earth! "The people that invented this calendar belonged to a higher civilization than ours," insisted Kiss.[4] According to his calculations, Tiwanaku was erected around 27,000 years before Christ's birth. This calendar, he maintained, was engraved in the stone by astronomers from the tertiary period and provides us with "incontrovertible, scientific evidence."[5]

1.2. Winged beings flank the central figure. Image courtesy of Tatjana Ingold, Solothurn, Switzerland.

Indeed, Hörbiger's followers actually did find evidence—in and around Tiwanaku—of some kind of global disaster. For instance, the remains of a large harbor, sea sediments at an altitude of 2.5 miles, volcanic ash mixed in with the mud from a flood of biblical proportions, and even fragments of bones from alleged giants. Not only that, all of these things originated from the time when our previous moon allegedly exploded, initially causing a ring of debris to form around the Earth that subsequently rained down catastrophically upon our planet. And let us not forget that—at least according to Hörbiger—this was not the first time. There had been many previous moons and many catastrophes. Hörbiger worked out that the amount of time that had elapsed during which the Earth was not orbited by any moon at all was 138,000 years. During that time, giant kings apparently reigned over the Earth. Then, around 14,000 years ago, the Earth captured our present moon and yet another catastrophe rolled over our mistreated globe: "From the north and the south, the seas flooded into the middle regions of the Earth; and in the north, on the plateaus that the newly captured moon had laid bare, the ice ages began."[6]

But has Hörbiger's World Ice Theory been completely refuted? Not quite, because giants did live on the Earth in days gone by—at least according to ancient records. But for now, let me tell you what I actually *know* on the subject.

Giants Roam the Earth

In Christianity's most holy book, the Bible, giants are mentioned as early as the Book of Genesis (Genesis 6:4): "There were giants on the earth in those days; and also after that, when the sons of God came in to the daughters of men, and they bore children to them: the same became mighty men, who were of old, men of renown."[7]

In the fifth book of the Pentateuch there is even mention of a mighty sarcophagus: "For only Og king of Bashan remained of the remnant of giants; behold, his bedstead was a bedstead of iron; is it not in Rabbath of the children of Ammon? Nine cubits was the length of it, and four cubits the breadth of it, after the cubit of a man" (Deuteronomy 3:11). (The Hebrew cubit was equivalent to 19 inches.) The same book mentions "a people great and tall, the sons of the Anakim" who God plans to destroy with a "consuming fire" (Deuteronomy, Chapters 2 & 3).

And we've all heard of the famous struggle between David and Goliath. In the Bible, it is described by the prophet Samuel (1 Samuel, Chapters 4–7):

> And there went out a champion from the camp of the Philistines, named Goliath, of Gath, whose height was six cubits and a span... and he was armed with a coat of mail; and the weight of the coat was five thousand shekels of brass...and the staff of his spear was like a weaver's beam; and his spear's head weighed six hundred shekels of iron...."

All but a very few of the gigantic "Anakites" were driven out by Joshua: "No Anakites were left in the land of the Israelites; only in Gaza, in Gath and Ashdod did any remain" (Joshua 11:22) and "In earlier times the name of Hebron had been Kiriath-arba, named after Arba, the greatest of the Anakim" (Joshua 15).

In the first Book of Chronicles, the reader can marvel at the story of how the last giant was finally killed:

> ...at which time Sibbechai the Hushathite slew Sippai, that was of the children of the giant...a man of great stature, whose fingers and toes were four and twenty, six on each hand, and six on each foot: and he also was the son of the giant. (Chapter 8) ...these were born to the giant in Gath; and they fell by the hand of David, and by the hand of his servants. (1 Chronocles 4 ff.)

Of course, the Bible is not the only source that confirms the existence of giants in previous ages. In the ancient texts on the legends of the Jews you can read: "There were the 'Emim' or the terrible ones, then the 'Rephaim' or giants, and also the 'Giborim' or the violent ones..."[8]

And giants are also mentioned in the 14th chapter of the book of the antediluvian prophet Enoch, one of the apocrypha. Here, the "Most High" reproaches his "fallen guardians of heaven": "Wherefore have ye left the high, holy, and eternal heaven, and lain with women, and defiled yourselves with the daughters of men and taken to yourselves wives, and done like the children of earth, and begotten giants (as your) sons?"[9]

In the Greek saga "The Argonautica," giants are mentioned frequently. Here's an example: On the Kapidag Peninsular, the Argonauts unwittingly climb a mountain to get a better view of their position. Heracles and a few men remain on board to guard the Argo. Suddenly, they are attacked by giants. But the monsters are unaware of Heracles who shoots and kills several of them from a distance with his arrows. "Their bodies have three pairs of nerved hands, like paws. The first pair hangs from their gnarled shoulders, the second and third pairs nestle up against their misbegotten hips...."[10]

These monsters crop up in many of the classic Greek sagas and legends. For instance, in Homer's Odyssey, when the hero battles against a giant on the Island of the Cyclops and burns out his only eye.[11] Nowadays, walls made of gigantic stone blocks are known as cyclops walls.

Monsters of varying kinds turn up in the Gilgamesh epic that was unearthed in Nineveh (in modern-day Iraq). The ancient clay tablets were part of the library of the Assyrian King Ashurbanipal. The story tells how Gilgamesh and his friend Enkidu climb the mountain of the gods together. Shortly before they reach their goal, they are confronted by a terrifying being called Humbaba. Humbaba has paws like a lion, his body is covered with iron scales, and his feet are armed with claws. The two brothers in arms shoot arrows at the monster and fling their throw-sticks, but everything simply bounces off. The "Park of the Gods" too is guarded by dreadful creatures. Namely, gigantic "scorpion-beings...

Trembling terror they inspire, the sight of them is death, their frightening aura sweeps over the mountains."[12] These monsters cannot be any ordinary creatures: They can talk and even give the two friends a stern warning.

The Sumerologist Professor Samuel Kramer even translated a passage from one of the cuneiform tablets in which a rape leads to the birth of a giant. Enlil impregnates Ninlil. She rejects his advances, but that doesn't stop Enlil from forcing her to his will: "...my vagina is too small. She does not understand coitus. My lips are too small...."[13]

You can also read about primitive giants in the Popol Vuh of the K'iche' Maya. They raged among mankind until the god Ah Mucenab unleashed a devastating inferno to wipe them out. Some survived and "wandered around lost in the dingy twilight. When they came across men there were desperate skirmishes."[14]

The Book of the Eskimos puts it succinctly: "In the old days there were giants on the Earth."[15]

To be honest, I could go on all day this way. There are quotes about giants in practically all of the ancient texts—regardless of which peoples compiled them. But humor me, and let me give you two more examples, as they are more precise than most of the popular legends. In the venerable book of the Ethiopian kings, the Kebra Negast, chapter 100 tells the following:

> And the daughters of Cain with whom the angels had coupled became with child, but were unable to bring forth their children, and they died. And some of the children who were in their wombs died, and some came forth; having split open the bellies of their mothers...and when they grew up and into manhood they became giants....[16]

The most unfathomable statement, however, can be found in the apocryphal Book of Baruch. Baruch actually states the number of giants who are said to have lived before the Flood: "God caused the deluge upon earth, and destroyed all flesh, and four hundred and nine thousand giants."[17] It remains a mystery as to where the venerable author got his figures from.

The allusions to giants in the ancient traditions are many and easy to find—for those who take the trouble to look. The difficulty is finding actual proof in terms of hard facts. Admittedly, many scientists have claimed to have made finds of giant bones or tools that could only have been made and used by giants, but they all remain controversial. For instance, German paleontologists Gustav von Koenigswald (1902–1982) and Franz Weidenreich (1873–1948) discovered several giant bones in apothecary shops in Hong Kong and China. Weidenreich even lectured on the subject to the American Ethnological Society in 1944.[18]

Hard Facts

Professor Denis Saurat, the renowned director of the Centre International d'Etudes Françaises in Nice, found hand axes weighing 8.4 pounds a little less than 4 miles south of Safita in Syria. And in Ain Fritissa in Eastern Morocco, he discovered some weighing 9.3 pounds (12.6 inches long and 8.7 inches wide)! In his expert opinion, axes of this size would only be suitable for use by giants.[19] Saurat supports the former existence of giants and even claimed that they could be responsible for the unexplained dolmens and huge menhirs that can be found throughout Europe. He also thought that it would account for the superhuman power required to build the cyclops walls that are dotted around the Mediterranean area. Bones from oversized early men were discovered as early as 1936 by German anthropologist L. Kohn-Larsen by Lake Eyasi in Tanzania. He even gave them a scientific name: Meganthropus africanus. Similar finds were made in Java (Meganthropus palaeojavanicus). The former delegate of the French Prehistoric Society, Dr. Louis Burkhalter, speaking in an article that appeared in the 1950 *Revue du Musée de Beyrouth* in Beirut, fully supported these bone findings: "I would like to make clear that the existence of giant humanoids in the Acheulean Epoch must be considered to be a scientifically proven fact."

In the middle of the last century, Australian archaeologist Dr. Rex Gilroy, director of the Mount York Natural History Museum in Bathurst, New South Wales, discovered huge prehistoric tools together with a skeleton and a molar tooth measuring 2.3 inches in length and 1.8 inches in breadth. He even found a huge footprint measuring 23.6 x 7.1 inches in the dried-up earth. Dr. Gilroy conjectured that the being that made this footprint would have had to have been 20 feet tall!

Another simply "impossible" finding involving massive footprints was made in Glen Rose, Texas. Here, in the riverbed of the Paluxy River, dinosaur footprints were discovered alongside those of giant human beings. All in the same sedimentary layer! Any anthropologist will tell you that that's just not possible: Dinosaurs and men never lived at the same time. Curiously, in this case it wasn't just one or two footprints; it was dozens! The direction of the dinosaur's flight is clearly identifiable—and the human footprints follow right behind as if they were chasing the beast.[20] The findings in Glen Rose ignited a heated scientific debate. The evolution theorists were united: dinosaur footprints and human footprints in the same sedimentary layer? It could only be a forgery. And they even ascribed this fakery to the creationists, those people who—especially in the United States—do not believe in Darwin's theory of evolution but rather that all life on Earth came about as a result of divine creation. The creationists themselves, on the other hand, vehemently denied that they had had anything to with it. The amazing thing about this scientific debate was the fact that the very few evolutionists who actually dared to make the trip to the Paluxy River to check out the discovery for themselves often ended up actually changing sides. People and dinosaurs at the same time? Impossible? In recent times, even the impossible seems to have become possible.

Renowned evolutionist biologist Professor Robert Martin from the Field Museum of Natural History (Chicago) is convinced that humans and dinosaurs lived at the same time: "Humans and other primates evolved around 90 million years ago. Accordingly, the ancestors of gorillas, chimpanzees and humans lived side by side with the dinosaurs and really only began their evolution after the dinosaur's extinction."[21]

Paleontologist Wolf-Dieter Heinrich from the Berlin Museum for Natural History actually found petrified remains from the Late Jurassic period. And he found them in the famous Tendaguru fossil layers in Tanzania—a site known for its dinosaur remains.

Professor Martin and his team conducted a number of molecular genetic tests that confirmed the extreme age of the bones. Professor Ulfur Arnason from the University of Lund in Sweden, also a molecular geneticist, has ascertained that "the most important split in the mammalian genealogical tree took place as early as the Mesozoic era."[22]

To conclude this short round of observations about giants in prehistory, I would like to share with you a strange story from King Solomon's times. In addition to a number of other women, the wise king—as we know—also had an intimate relationship with the Queen of Sheba (or, as she is also known in Arabic, Balqis). The last meeting between Solomon and the Queen of Sheba took place in Tadmor, the city of palms. (Tadmor was later known as Palmyra, an oasis town in the north of the Syrian desert.) The wasteful Solomon had a huge mausoleum erected in the city for his great love. Muhammed al-Hassan, biographer of the prophet Mohammed, reported that Caliph Walid the first (705–715 AD) had found a grave with the inscription "This is the grave and the bier of the pious Balqis, wife of Solomon." The caliph had the grave opened. When he saw what was inside his blood froze, and he ordered that the grave be closed and never again opened. On top of the tomb, he erected a large building as a warning. What on earth had horrified the caliph so? The tomb of Balqis was the grave of a giant![23]

Maybe the controversial giants of Hörbiger's World Ice Theory were not so spurious after all. He could have taken his information from the ancient records that, after all, were all available in those days. And let's not forget—whether we like it or not—Darwin's evolution never ran as smoothly as his theory would have us believe. In their well-researched 1,000-page work, *Forbidden Archaeology*, authors Michael Cremo and Richard Thompson document a whole host of anthropological inconsistencies that certainly do not fit in with the idea of linear evolution.[24] The book has, incomprehensibly, been ignored by both archaeo- and anthropologists. The preciseness of the sources and proofs, however, is mighty impressive.

The Origin of the Moon?

Now, let's not forget that Hans Hörbiger also maintained in his World Ice Theory that there had been several different moons circling around the Earth, and that the current one had only been in orbit for around 14,000 years. The various moons were the real reason for the rise and fall of the many different cultures, he postulated, including the culture from Tiwanaku. Absurd? Don't we have conclusive evidence about the Moon and its heritage? After all, Americans have even brought moon rock back home with them, haven't they? (Just for the skeptics: I know all those books that claim that the Americans never went to the Moon and that the landings shown on TV were nothing but hokum cooked up in the desert and various TV studios. That kind of anti-Americanism is easy enough to disprove. U.S. astronauts deposited a measuring plate on the Moon that is, to this day, homed in on via laser from the Earth. It is used to measure the exact distance between the Earth and the Moon. And what's more, further Moon landings are planned by the Chinese and Japanese. Of course, they will find all the junk left lying around by the Americans on their previous visits. As usual, none of the unbelievers from the "Anti-Moon-Landing League" will bother to apologize to the Americans. (I am personally acquainted with several of the men who worked on the NASA Moon Program, starting with Wernher von Braun, Hermann Obeth, Willi Ley, Harry Ruppe, Ernst Stuhlinger—all of them the proud bearers of the title of either professor or doctor—right up to chief engineer Joseph Blumrich. All of them were honorable men—without exception. Not one single one of them would have been involved with any kind of global Moon deception.)

So, do we know how the Moon was created or how old it is? Have Hörbiger's fantasies finally been laid to rest?

There are a number of theories about the origin of the Moon:[25]

- **The fission hypothesis.** The rotation of the proto-Earth generated centrifugal forces that flung out a large chunk of its mass into space. This coalesced to form the Moon.

- **The many-moons hypothesis.** Several smaller satellites were caught in the Earth's gravitational field. These collided and formed today's moon.

- **The capture hypothesis.** The Earth and the Moon arose independently of each other. At some stage the Earth "caught" the Moon in its gravitational field.

- **The co-formation hypothesis.** The Earth and the Moon formed together from the primordial gloop at the same time and place; the Moon itself forming from the material surrounding the proto-Earth.

- **The giant impact hypothesis.** The Earth collided with a huge Mars-sized body. The matter that was thrown out into space came together to form the Moon.

Whichever is correct, the latest research from the Swiss Federal Institute of Technology (ETH) and the Universities of Oxford (England), Cologne (Germany), and Münster (Germany) all concludes that the Moon was created many millions of years ago.[26] How does one come up with such a venerable age?

It's all down to the levels of the isotope wolfram-182, which is formed as a result of the decomposition of the radioactive isotope hafnium. Hafnium decomposes completely in 60 million years. This is a physical fact. Scientists at the Institute for Isotope Geology at the ETH Zürich examined moon rocks that the U.S. astronauts had brought with them back to Earth. They measured minuscule amounts of wolfram-182, which allowed them to ascertain the age on the basis of decomposed hafnium. The larger the differences in the wolfram-182, the older the rock has to be. The result was an age of X million years[27] and tends to support the "giant impact hypothesis," which states that the Earth and the Moon are two heavenly bodies that collided with each other millions of years ago.

Assuming we believe these latest results, then Hörbiger was certainly wrong, and our Moon hasn't been orbiting the Earth for only 14,000 years. So it cannot be responsible for the destruction of Tiwanaku. Nevertheless, whether it was the Moon or not, it can certainly be shown that the Earth has been hit by abrupt climatic catastrophes in its past. These are revealed by examining sediments or glacial erratics (large chunks of rocks deposited by melting glaciers at the end of the last ice age; the foothills of the Alps are full of them). (By the way, those glaciers melted many thousands of years ago without the help of today's greenhouse gases—a fact that is often glossed over in current discussions.)

There have even been cosmic impacts during Earth's history. Meteorites may have collided with the Earth at certain times or fallen into its oceans and triggered horrendous floods around the world. The only thing is: The cause of all these things—as we now know—cannot have been the Moon. So Hörbiger's followers will need to think again.

There is, however, one point that still remains open—something that Hörbiger simply came up with intuitively and that has recently again been the subject of some debate. Hörbiger claimed that everything in the cosmos was subject to an overarching process of evolution—that the entire universe was a "living organism" in which every constituent part has an influence on every other part. And indeed, elementary particles didn't just acquire their confusing characteristics from nowhere, but rather through their interaction with other objects, such as Higgs particles. Particles are—as the word implies—not independent objects; they are a "part" of something else. Every particle reflects the whole, and the universe consists of particles that it has created itself. This simple truth has led astrophysicists to the (at first glance absurd) question: Is the universe a living organism?

The Universe: A Living Organism?

What or perhaps even who is the universe? Is God simply a manifestation of the entire cosmos? Questions like these have been a part of religious philosophy for millennia, and were not concocted by Hörbiger. In modern astrophysics the "being of the universe" is treated just as it is in religion—the difference is, however, that cosmologists do not claim to represent faith but scientific opinion. Professor Paul Davies, a quantum physicist and cosmologist at the Arizona State University, has published several articles on the subject as well as controversial books such as *The Accidental Universe, The Mind of God, About Time,* and *The Goldilocks Enigma.*[28]

Another brilliant exponent of this "God-as-universe" hypothesis is the American James Gardner. Talking at international conventions and symposia, he astounds and amazes his listeners with his cool logic and provocative statements such as the following:

Every kid knows that the universe is an environment that is hostile
to mankind. But if you look a little bit deeper, you'll see that that's
not true. The universe is a very hospitable place![29]

James Gardner begins his presentations with the origin of the universe and proves that this very hospitability was a constituent element of the Big Bang itself. All of the components—which later developed into atoms, subatomic particles, molecules, and even life forms—were already present at the time of the Big Bang. Looking at it from this point of view, the development and proliferation of life forms in the cosmos did not happen on a random basis, but was rather a natural part of universal evolution. The aim of the universe is to fill the entire cosmos with intelligent life. Thus, we continuously observe the birth of new universes. Every black hole that swallows a Milky Way, spits it back out again in a new Big Bang somewhere and somewhen else. There's a kind of cosmic reproduction going on: New "baby universes" are being born. Highly advanced hyper-civilizations then seed these baby universes with life. This "message of life" is spreading through the entire cosmos; we humans are simply a part of it. This is one insight that I have shared in many of my books, long before I had ever read James Gardner's wonderful research.[30] So where did *my* insight come from? Well, it's no coincidence, claims the controversial James Gardner. It is the "memes" that are responsible for this proliferation.[31] Unlike genes, memes are information particles that spread like viruses. Whereas genes pass on hereditary information (DNA), memes transmit information in a more disembodied manner—directly from brain to brain, uninterrupted, day in day out, and throughout the entire universe. Every time I give a lecture, I "infect" other brains with my memes. (The same thing, dear reader, is happening to you right now as you read these very words.)

Hörbiger may have scored a few lucky points with his World Ice Theory—for instance, on the possible existence of giants in the dim and distant past, or the flooding of ancient sites as a result of global catastrophes—but in most other respects he was way off base. The Moon of today has been around for a lot longer than 14,000 years, for instance. Then I ask myself, how did Hörbiger come up with the idea that the entire universe is some kind of cosmic life form? That was considered crazy talk back in those days. Was it just his megalomania, or did it have something to do with the memes?

The Discovery of Tiwanaku

People have been streaming to Tiwanaku for centuries. The earliest reports on the subject came from the Spanish chronicler Pedro Cieza de León, who visited in 1549.

Tiaguanaco no es pueblo muy grande, pero es mentado por los grandes edificios que tiene....

...Tiwanaku is not a small village, rather it is famous for its grandiose buildings...a short distance from a hill stand two stone statues shaped as men...they are so large that they look like giants ...but the thing that elicits the greatest amount of wonder is the size [of the stone slabs; author's addition], which are so huge we cannot understand how men could ever have moved them. Many

1.3. The platforms of Puma Punku. Image courtesy of Tatjana Ingold, Solothurn, Switzerland.

of these platforms have been worked in various ways.... There are also stone slabs with doorways, all made from a single block...we do not comprehend with which tools such work could have been achieved...what's more, the blocks must have been even greater in size before they were worked.... No one understands how these great weights could ever have been moved.... I have been assured that these constructions were already there before the Inca ruled, and much of what the Inca later erected in Cuzco had been inspired by what they had seen in Tiwanaku.... In the presence of Juan Varagas, I asked the natives whether these buildings had been erected during the age of the Incas: they laughed and answered, the buildings had been there for many years before the Incas began their rule. These structures, they assured me, and they knew this with certainty from their forefathers, had been built in a single night, constructed by beings whose provenance they did not know.... And may the fame of these things remain intact throughout the universe... (...y hacen que vuela la fama de las cosas que suceden por el universo...) There were none still living who knew this unearthly site as anything other than ruins ....[32]

Some 400 years ago, Garcilaso de la Vega, too, stood before the ruins of the mighty walls and platforms, only some of which remain today. (This is because the Bolivians blew up the millennia-old slabs to make stone for building.)

In Book 1, Chapter 23, of his work on the subject Garcilaso de la Vega wrote of the inexplicable site:

I looked in wonder at a great wall built of such mighty stones that we could not imagine which earthly power could have been used to accomplish such a feat.... The natives maintain that the buildings were there before the Incas.... They do not know who the builders were, but know with some degree of certainty from their ancestors that all these wonders were erected in a single night....[33]

Juan de Betanzos, another Spanish chronicler of that time, claimed to know that it was the creator "Con-Tici Viracocha" who also created the sun, Moon, and stars: "And in that same night of the people, he personally built Tiwanaku."[34]

1.4. Sections of the platform at Puma Punku. Image courtesy of Tatjana Ingold, Solothurn, Switzerland.

According to this version, the gods—however you wish to interpret that term—were involved in Tiwanaku's construction. One thing all of the chroniclers are agreed on: The mighty complex was built "in a single night."

In 1572, Cristóbal de Molina was working as a priest and doctor in the Indio hospital in Cuzco. He had intensive contact with the indigenous peoples and diligently wrote down all their religious lore. Hans Hörbiger could have used his writings as a source for his World Ice Theory, as Molina wrote that Manco Capac was the first Inca and that the "flood" story was already well known by educated Indios in pre-Christian times. According to their legends, all life had been destroyed and the floodwaters covered even the highest mountains. Only one man and one woman survived the flood "in a box."[35] The creator, they said, had delivered this pair to Tiwanaku where he started to create new animals, fish, and birds.

I'd have no problem quoting at least 50 pages from the age of the Spanish conquistadores and I'd always come to the same conclusion: Anyone who visited the ruins of Tiwanaku 400 years ago and stood in front of neighboring Puma Punku would have felt overawed by the mighty constructions. These days, you might even say overwhelmed. A hundred years later, Antonio de Castro y del Castillo, who was Bishop of La Paz in 1651, summed it up perfectly:

> Although it was once supposed that the ruins had been the work of the Incas, as fortresses for their wars, now it is clear that they are, in fact, *of antediluvian origin....* [author's emphasis] Had it been the Inca's work, buried so deep, not even the Spanish would have been capable of creating such a wonderful and momentous building...[36]

Miguel Balboa, a chronicler and priest who settled in Peru in 1566, wrote that even the Inca Huayna Capac had viewed the ruins of Tiwanaku "with awe and wonder."[37]

A Stony Problem

The astonishment and wonder of those men who stood before the ruins of Tiwanaku all those centuries ago also left later visitors shaking their heads in awe and reverence. But that wasn't all there was to see: Another part of the Tiwanaku complex consists of a series of inexplicable monster-sized stone blocks, known as Puma Punku. They are situated just a few miles southwest of Tiwanaku—and I would like to tell you now: if you ever visit Tiwanaku, don't miss Puma Punku! Don't be put off by any excuses from tired tour guides. Whereas Tiwanaku has, to a small extent, been reconstructed, this is not possible in Puma Punku. The stone platforms are simply too heavy and too huge. Thanks to Hörbiger's World Ice Theory and the racist Nazi philosophies of that time, Puma Punku has been scandalously ignored in the modern archaeological literature. This is how South America's mysterious Puma Punku is treated in one sumptuous anthology—in just a couple of lines of text:

In the southwestern corner of Tiwanaku stand the large pyramids known as Puma Punku. Their upper platforms form two flat areas at different heights, both of which can be reached by ascending several flights of steps. On one of the platforms a temple may have stood, with three large portals built in the style of the sun gate.[38]

That's not just meager; it's also wrong. Puma Punku was never a pyramid and doesn't present itself as one today either, and the so-called "sun gate"—well that's another subject entirely and has nothing to do with the platforms of Puma Punku. (I'll get back to that later.)

In the first half of the 19th century, French paleontologist Alice Charles Victor d'Orbigny (1802–1857) traveled to South America. In 1833, he stood before the ruins of Puma Punku and reported on the "mighty portals that stand on horizontal stone slabs."[39] He measured the length of one of the uninterrupted platforms as 131 feet. These days, however, there are no more interconnected slabs: They are all broken, smashed, or simply ravaged by time. Despite the fact that the Bolivian Army was still using the slabs at Puma Punku for its target practise right up until the 1940s, the stones that remain are still sufficient to leave

1.5. A view of the so-called desk. Author's own image.

you breathless. In 1869, Swiss travel writer Johann Jakob von Tschudi stumbled over the ruins of Puma Punku and wrote: "On the way to Puma Punku, we came upon a field with a strange monolith, around 5 feet high and roughly 5.5 feet wide. At its base, it is around 2 feet thick, and at its peak 1.5 feet. It features two row of slots or compartments. The monolith is known as *El Escritorio,* the desk."[40]

Whoever it was that dubbed this block "the desk"—because the various compartments do actually remind you of drawers—was barking up the wrong tree. This block is made of andesite and probably served as a support for stone struts. Even as a specialist in Stone Age mysteries, Puma Punku always leaves me breathless. And I've been there 16 times! This Puma Punku and neighboring Tiwanaku are a panorama of another culture. Mighty blocks of andesite and diorite (a gray-green plutonic rock that is incredibly hard and resistant to weathering), are strewn around. There is absolutely no granite there. The monoliths have been worked with such a precision, honed and polished as if they had been created in a workshop equipped with modern tools such as stainless steel milling machines and diamond-tipped drills. Exquisitely precise channels, around a quarter of an inch wide and roughly a third of an inch deep, cut at right angles—something that simply would not be possible with Stone Age tools—run over the diorite monoliths. (See image 1.6 on page 48.) Nothing here fits in with the image of a primitive Stone Age culture. Puma Punku was witness to some impressive high-tech—and that can be proved.

Even before Hans Hörbiger started harassing the scientific community with his World Ice Theory, two other German scientists visited Tiwanaku and Puma Punku. Max Uhle (1856–1944) was an archaeologist. He is known as the "Father of Peruvian Archaeology." He met geologist and explorer Alphons Stübel (1835–1904) at the Royal Zoological and Anthropological-Ethnographical Museum in Dresden. The two learned men were soon friends and colleagues and, in 1892, they published an incomparable standard work: *Die Ruinenstätte von*

1.6. An extremely fine groove runs over the polished diorite block. Author's own image.

Tiahuanaco im Hochlande des alten Perú (*The Ruins of Tiahuanaco in the Highlands of Ancient Peru*).[41] This work, which is only to be found in the larger libraries these days and is usually not lent out, is 23 inches tall and 15 inches wide, and weighs around 22 pounds! Alphons Stübel noted the precise measurements that they had made in Tiwanaku and Puma Punku, and the archaeologist Max Uhle carefully collected the entire canon of existing writings on the subject of the mysterious ruins. His text is filled with footnotes, notices, and remarks.

Even back then, Tiwanaku lay in ruins. Plundered and cannibalized by robbers and state organizations that transported the perfectly polished blocks off to goodness-knows-where and used them to build houses. This is where, for example, the entire raw material for the village church in Tiwanaku came from, as well as its enclosure wall and the courtyards all around. Monoliths were smashed, precisely worked blocks were converted, and millennia-old columns were adapted to fit in with the church's architecture. So it's hardly surprising that today's reconstruction work in Tiwanaku is only able to give hints of the site's former glories. Nevertheless, Stübel was able to measure a rectangle 394 feet long (from north to south) and 371 feet wide (east to west). At the front of this rectangle stood a half-broken gateway made of light-gray, andesitic lava, 9.9 feet high, 12.5 feet wide, and nearly 20 inches thick. It is known today as the "Gateway of the Sun." Chiseled into the stone are 48 winged beings flanking a main figure on the left and right. Max Uhle wrote:

"In them [the winged beings; author's addition] we see the most precious legacy of a long-forgotten epoch in religious history.... The mythology in this depiction reveals itself in the wings of the beings that surround the figure in the middle.... And this central figure, too, can be nothing less than some kind of divine being, not least because of the corona surrounding it and the other wondrous signs. It is the sovereign God, to whom homage is being paid by a host of winged, heavenly servants. It almost seems as though the frieze running along the bottom was intended to transpose this homage scene from the Earth onto a heavenly setting....[42]

1.7. The front side of the Gateway of the Sun, from around 1910. Public domain image.

This spontaneous interpretation of the sun gate comes from the year 1877. All of the following academics of

1.8. An accurate drawing of the central figure, from around 1910. Public domain image.

that epoch, such as Professor Arthur Posnansky, Dr. Edmund Kiss, and Dr. Hans Schindler Bellamy, analyzed the figures on the sun gate and assumed that they represented the most phenomenal calendar in the world. (That's another thing I'll come back to later.)

Stühle and Uhle were astonished by the quality of the stone material used at Tiwanaku and Puma Punku. I quote:

> The types of andesite worked here display such a degree of hardness and durability that we must surely categorize them as some of most difficult of all to work.... Bearing in mind the characteristics of the majority of the worked material, we are faced with not only an architectural but also a technical problem here at the site of the ruins. It would seem that the quality of the work here is out of all proportion to the technical means available to the ancient Peruvians.[43]

These sentences come from Alphons Stübel, a geologist by trade and an expert who—we can be fairly sure—was well acquainted with the degree of hardness of the stones. Diorite—for example—a gray-green plutonic rock, has a hardness grade of 8. The hardness grade is a measurement of the resistance of a solid body to being penetrated by another body. The hardness of minerals is measured on the Mohs scale (named after Friedrich Mohs, 1773–1839). Any solid material has a lower degree of hardness than a material that can be used to scratch it, and a higher one than any material it can scratch. Take a look at this: Diamonds, the hardest minerals on Earth, have a hardness grade of 10. Diamonds cannot be scratched by stones like granite. In order to work diorite with the kind of unbelievable precision that can be seen in Puma Punku, you would need far more advanced tools than just stone axes. (See image 1.9 on page 52.) The tools that were used must have been at least as hard as, if not harder than, diorite. To maintain anything else is just humbug!

1.9. Every piece is polished. Author's own image.

Feeble Excuses

That's it exactly! There's certainly something rotten in the Kingdom of Denmark! For a start, because of the tools that simply don't fit in with this Stone Age culture, and secondly because of the complex technical plans that would have been necessary. Honestly, today's archaeology really can't take the risk of looking at the problem, because it would open a real can of worms. Intentionally. Even back in the age of the Spanish conquistadores, so-called "comités" were set up that were given the task of systematically destroying everything that alluded to the "heathen religion." The priests' fanatism was insatiable. The comités consisted of people who were familiar with the conditions in the area. Often, the sons of the tribal chiefs and sun priests were forced to join these comités and seek out the ancient shrines. Under the leadership of the Catholic priests, everything was destroyed that was in any way destroyable. It was a systematic erasure of the hated heathen culture. Thousands of statues and temples built by the Inca and from pre-Inca times were smashed, and the rubble was thrown down the mountainside. The only religious symbol that was allowed was the sign of the cross. And when this religious zeal was finally sated, then came the stone plunderers looking for building material for streets, churches, and houses. Maybe the Tiwanaku builders suspected the dangers of blind, religious zeal and intentionally left behind a few signs for eternity.

Tiwanaku is said to have been built "in a single night"—according to the chroniclers. It involved unknown builders, unknown tools, and unknown draftsmen. One of the helpful gods was called "Viracocha," but "Ticsiviracocham Con Ticsi Viracocha and Pachayachachic are one and the same figure."[44] According to Stübel and Uhle, the word can be separated into its Quechua components. *Cocha* means sea; *vira* is fat or foam. Put it together, and you end up with "foam sea." Linguistic scientist E.W. Middendorf, who published four volumes of the Quechua and Aymara languages around 150 years ago and is recognized as one of the world's great authorities on Indio languages, comes up with another interpretation. He translates "Con Ticsi Viracocha" as *"God of the liquid lava sea"* [author's emphasis].[45] Here *con* =god, *ticsi* =lava, and *cocha* = sea. Johann Jakob Tschudi translated this correspondingly as "Sea of the origin and end of all things."[46]

Does the name "God of the liquid lava sea" bring us any closer to the secret of this Viracocha?

After Stübel and Uhle had paved the way for serious research in Tiwanaku, a number of other scientists from various different faculties picked up on the subject. Around the turn of the century, Tiwanaku and Puma Punku were the very epitome of a world mystery—alongside Egypt, of course. The problem was that Egypt was a lot closer for the British, French, and German archaeologists who preferred to dig around in the desert sands. Very few chose to take the arduous journey to the High Andes of Peru and Bolivia. Let's not forget that Tiwanaku lies at an altitude of some 13,000 feet. The air is thin and the way up is difficult. Today's tourists have it much easier. A jet brings them to La Paz, the capital of Bolivia. From there, it's just an hour and a half on the now fully paved road to Tiwanaku and Puma Punku. The altitude hasn't changed, however, and if you choose to make the trip, don't try to do too much on your first few days. It takes a couple of days for your blood cells to acclimate to the different altitude.

Posnansky: A Fanatic?

One man who decided he did want to know more was Arthur Posnansky, the Royal Bavarian professor of geodesic engineering. He worked from 1904 to 1945 in Tiwanaku. The place fascinated him so much that, soon after he got there, he decided to remain in Bolivia, and over the years he was lauded with one honorary academic title after the other. Posnansky was: President of the Geographic Society of La Paz; president of the Archaeological Society of Bolivia; director of the Tiwanaku Institute for Anthropology; Ethnography and Early History; member of the New York Academy of Sciences; and so on and so on. From 1910 onward, practically nothing happened in the field of Bolivian and Peruvian archaeology unless Arthur Posnansky had given it the go ahead. He was respected, honored, and hated—all in all a very controversial person. Posnansky wrote four scientific treatises on Tiwanaku, or the "cradle of humanity," as he called it.[47] He despised, mocked, and scorned archaeologist Max Uhle, even calling him an illusionist, counterfeiter, and fantasist, this last in a pamphlet written to discredit Max Uhle.[48]

Posnansky was the first person to ascertain the exact geographic position of Tiwanaku: 16 degrees, 33 minutes, and 7 seconds south, and 68 degrees, 40 minutes and 24 seconds west of Greenwich. Posnansky cursed the unprofessional destruction of the ruins by an excavator named Georges Courty and claimed that this same indiscriminate and cavalier Georges Courty, who had carried out excavations in Tiwanaku in 1903, was nothing more than a grave robber and had caused more destruction than in any of the long ages that had passed. The indigenous peoples, according to Posnansky, had named their main temple "Akapana," as their forefathers had done. In the ancient Aymara language this meant "the place where the observers dwell." That's something we really ought to keep in mind, don't you think?

According to Posnansky, Tiwanaku had experienced no "decadent period. And those that claim such nonsense have never really studied this prehistoric metropolis.... Tiwanaku is the greatest sun temple ever to be constructed by mankind—not just in South America, but in the whole world."[49]

That was no flamboyant comparison: Posnansky was well acquainted with the structures in Egypt. In Tiwanaku he found countless signs that pointed to a connection between Heaven and Earth. He deciphered depictions of stars and other heavenly bodies and noted that one of the large statues that was found in Tiwanaku carried the name Pachamama, which meant no less than "Mother of the Cosmos." (*Pacha* means "cosmos" in Aymara.) This statue bears two of the same winged beings on its breast that can be seen on the sun gate. On its back is a series of phenomenally delicate illustrations engraved millimeter for millimeter, as if the hand of the

1.10. This statue is known as Pachamama. Image courtesy of Tatjana Ingold, Solothurn, Switzerland.

artist were guided by some kind of intricate stencil and he were using a drill of dental precision. The statue is now the pride and joy of the Open-air Museum in La Paz. Among the engravings, Posnansky discovered the most perfect calendar, which not only chronicled the passing of the year, but also the phases of the moon.

The same applied to the engravings on the Gateway of the Sun. The "priest-astronomers" (Posnansky) knew how to represent the winter and summer solstices, and also the equinoxes, the daily position of the Moon, and even the "heavenly equator" down to the finest detail ("y el eje vertical de estas dos Figuras representa el Ecuador Celeste").[50]

Posnansky was pulled along by his own excitement and enthusiasm. He was acquainted with all of the literature that had been written about Tiwanaku, knew the legends and lore of the Incas, could speak Aymara and Quechua fluently, and was determined to find the answer to one key question: How was all this possible? He often doubted his own discoveries, consulted with other scientists, and was still forced to come to the same conclusion—namely that Tiwanaku must be viewed a kind of prehistoric metropolis, built before the last great flood by beings that were somehow way more advanced than any kind of Stone Age man had any right to be. For Posnansky, the Gateway of the Sun was just the centerpiece of a fantastic wall filled with calendrical depictions. ("...La Puerta del Sol es unicamente la Parte central de un formidable muro de inscriptiones calendograficas....."[51])

This means that the priest-astronomers must have taken the precession of the Earth into account. (Precession refers to variations in the inclination of a planet's rotational axis. The Earth's precession cycle lasts around 25,800 years.) Posnansky identified three construction periods at Tiwanaku and noted that parts of Puma Punku at least belonged to the oldest of these—this oldest period was also, paradoxically, the most technically perfect, contrary to any rules of technological evolution. As we all know, at the beginning it's always quite primitive: Tools and techniques have to be developed. From generation to generation, small advances are made and skills improve. This only applies to a limited extent at Tiwanaku, because in one corner of the complex lies Puma Punku—built with inexplicable technology. Later generations simply tried to extend the complex with poorer-quality tools.

Based on his *astronomical calculations,* Posnansky dated the second period as being at least 10,000 years before Christ, and the oldest at around 15,450 BC. This was long before New Grange (Ireland), Stonehenge (England), or any kind of Egyptian or Sumerian culture. At least, it was if we accept established archaeological teachings.

But although Arthur Posnansky was often overtaken by his own enthusiasm, he was anything but a fantasist. He was a true researcher in body and soul: He didn't simply base all his work on his own discoveries and theories, but rather called regularly on the wisdom of other astronomers, geologists, and so forth. In this way, he was able to ascertain that the fauna and flora present during the building of the first stage of Tiwanaku must have changed radically: "This can be clearly shown by the remains of sea life and the silt sediments by Lake Titicaca."[52] Posnansky searched for the quarry from which the large stone blocks came and found it around 40 miles from the site of the ruins in the volcanic slopes of "Kjapphia" (now known as "Cerro de Skapia") near Zepita on the Peruvian side of the border. Here, a number of various different types of andesite could be found. (Andesite forms from cooled volcanic magma.)

Then Posnansky was confronted with another problem: How did the blocks get all the way to Tiwanaku? The most plausible solution involved specially built roads on a very solid foundation. Rollers would have then been used to get the 200-ton slabs moving. Then came the ships. Posnansky maintained there was once—"without a shadow of doubt"[53]—a canal system. The fact that there was water around can be shown geologically. Tiwanaku itself was sited on a harbor. But that was a long, long time ago in a prehistoric epoch.

Posnansky was the first person to postulate a complicated and perfectly designed canalization system, including piping that—to this day—looks as if it were cast in modern concrete. (See figure 1.11.) In addition to this, there existed—in Puma Punku in particular—a number of underground chambers created from andesite blocks that were as perfectly fitted into each other as a waterproof Swiss watch. Posnansky often demonstrated this to his incredulous visitors by pouring bucket after bucket of water into the closed rooms.

Today's tourists don't get to see these subterranean rooms. They are still there, but they have been filled in.

1.11. These pieces of pipe look almost as if they were cast in concrete (photo from 1967). Author's own image.

There was one problem for which Posnansky could find no solution:

…Hay otra cosa curiosa.…

There is one other puzzling thing. At the center of the Sun Temple in Tiwanaku, in other words in the most important part of the existing ruins, I discovered a cut block around one meter wide and two meters long. This was, without a doubt, where the priest-astronomers had once placed the Gateway of the Sun in the center of their gigantic calendrical wall. The strange thing about it is the fact that this central block, lying at the holiest point in the complex, is made of a completely different kind of stone than the rest of the ruins. It is an uncommonly ugly stone…. For the lay person, it looks as if it were put together from many other particles, but I suspect that this is a kind of hard trachyte with seams of another volcanic rock making it look like a conglomerate of different stones. I would like to repeat: this stone was not used anywhere else—neither for the statues, nor for the platforms.[54]

Maybe, but this can only be speculation, this was some kind of "concrete casting," and—again maybe—was where the urns lay that the constructors left for the generations of the distant future. I have looked for this "uncommonly ugly" block and have not been able to locate it—not in the Open-air Museum of La Paz, nor in the junkyard of Puma Punku.

Arthur Posnansky was somewhat perplexed by his first views of Puma Punku: "One is somewhat shocked by that which one sees and it seems almost as if one were standing in front of a cyclopean workshop." ("En el primer momento unoqueda aturdido al ver algo que pareceria taller de ciclopos.")[55] Later, Posnansky allocated the rubble yard of Puma Punku to the first and oldest period. Although he suspected that Puma Punku was some kind of Moon temple, he finally conceded that the ruins will probably always remain an enigma. The translation of Puma Punku, by the way, is "gateway of the puma." Posnansky asked the older men about their histories, and they assured him that the original name had been "Winay Marca," which meant "eternal city." An ideal name for the ruins of Puma Punku.

The quintessence of Posnansky's research culminates in the following:

It is attestable beyond doubt that the main temple [of Tiwanaku; author's addition] was an observatory which was aligned to the astronomical meridian and also, at the same time, an ingeniously devised stone calendar.... And the hieroglyphic and symbolic inscriptions on the sun gate are nothing less than a detailed description of the calendar's various functions.[56]

Climate Change? Nothing New

Posnansky's findings were not accepted blindly—even back in those days. Like Hans Hörbiger, Posnansky was convinced by the idea of "glacial epochs." He had discovered an ancient building with walls that were almost 12 feet thick in a bay at Lake Titicaca. He wrote about it in the Bolivian daily *El Diario* from July 14, 1931: "It is well known that the Earth has gone through several ice ages during which broad lakes and meltwater accumulated that once covered the entire Bolivian-Peruvian high plain...this building must have been built before the ice age at a time when Lake Titicaca was not as big as it is now...."

Everyone has heard of the concept of climate change—nowadays! But back in Posnansky's day they were already talking about climate changes—in the plural! We're not talking about examining ozone holes—we didn't have the technology back then—or taking ice cores in the Antarctic. A hundred years ago, it was all about picks and shovels and good sense. The results were the same as now. Edmund Kiss, who admittedly was a follower of Hörbiger and researched in Tiwanaku after Posnansky, confirmed what others after him were also forced to concede: "The fact that Tiwanaku was once completely under water is certain. The large stairway in Tiwanaku is covered in a thin layer of calcium that was must have been deposited by water. It is so firmly attached that you need to take a knife to scratch off a sample...."[57]

Kiss believed that Tiwanaku had been destroyed by a flood and cited bone remains as his proof:

> The bones of people and animals, including many species that are now extinct, lie in wild confusion in Tiwanaku's alluvial sediments. This bone sediment is at one point 3.5 meters thick.... At one point, the railroad track runs through a gully with sides 3.5 meters high and this does not even break through the bone sediment. Under the rails, the same sediment can be seen, consisting of millions upon millions of smaller and larger bones, fragments of glazed ceramic malachite pearls and much more....[58]

Like Posnansky, Edmund Kiss also confirmed the existence of "tide-marks" that ran along the cliffs for many miles. Posnansky had assumed that the highlands of Bolivia had been flooded many times because the Earth's axis had changed pushing the entire Andes region upward. Kiss, however, rejected this standpoint. But he remained convinced that Tiwanaku had been flooded at some point. The attentive observer Kiss also noted that it was not only the village church of Tiwanaku that had been built from stone stolen from the ruins of Tiwanaku, but also the great cathedral of the capital La Paz.

An Ice Age Calendar

Edmund Kiss then concentrated on the depictions on the Gateway of the Sun. He noted that—without exception—the winged forms on the frieze all had just four fingers on each hand and only three toes on each foot. After many years of study, Kiss came up with a theory that was so oddball that he felt compelled to apologize before even mentioning it:

> ...let me beg you now, do not just set the book down. And let me also implore you, after reading the information which I am about to impart...not to call the doctor and beg him to prescribe the poor author a course of cold-water treatments. He assures you that he is indeed healthy and it is not easy for him to proffer his broad shoulders for the inevitable crushing laughter to come....[59]

At least the man had a sense of humor! So which impossible theory are we talking about here?

1. That the Gateway of the Sun in Tiwanaku is a calendar marking 12 periods of the year. It also displays the solstices and the equinoxes.

2. Each of these 12 periods has 24 days. Only the months February and April have 25.

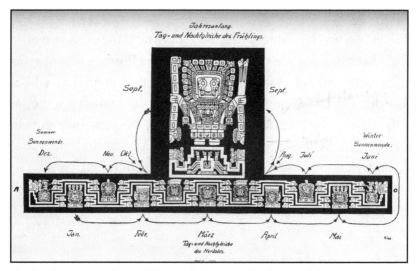

1.12. An excerpt from Edmund Kiss's calendar. Public domain image.

3. Each of these days has 30 hours.

4. Each of these hours has 22 minutes.

At first glance, it does seem a little crazy. But Kiss backed up every single infinitesimal detail on the frieze of the Gateway of the Sun. ("Frieze" here means the *lower* part, not the 48 winged forms above.) Kiss calculated backward and forward; he neglected nothing—not even the tiniest detail: Everything was correct. Every tiny circle had an exact meaning; every "puma head" or "snake tail" fit exactly into his calendar theory. Kiss showed pictures of the frieze to many of his scientific colleagues, and asked them to count it for themselves and disprove his calculations. Not one of them could. It only worked, though, on the premise that a year actually did have 12 months made up of 24 days at 30 hours, and every hour of 22 minutes. Did the ancient residents of Tiwanaku really use a calendar like this? And if they did, when? How many thousands of years ago? Before the last ice age?

I would love to give you Edmund Kiss's variation on the calendar right here, but I would have to quote at least 30 pages from his book, and that's just not possible. Those of you who really want to know will just have to go and seek out the book for yourselves. It always helps to have a picture, to give yourself an idea of what Kiss was actually talking about. Kiss himself concluded:

> Can it really be a coincidence? Or is it the deluded invention of a man who—come what may—is determined to decipher the calendar on the Gateway of the Sun in Tiwanaku? Well, in that case the number of coincidences is piling up at an alarming rate! No, the interpretation of these pictograms is not forced: it came about almost of itself as soon as the hieroglyphs on the base had been deciphered. The three references indicating where the lunar cycles are to be found depending on the year and the month, as well as how they are to be counted, are of such a compelling logic that the way they are depicted on the calendar can only described ingenious.[60]

Was everything that the worthy doctors Edmund Kiss and Arthur Posnansky claimed to have discovered all just bunk? Well, put it this way: They weren't the only ones. After the Second World War a number of others followed. And let's not forget that we really should treat these two as completely separate figures, not least because of their wildly different ideologies. Hans Hörbiger, propagator of the World Ice Theory, was known as a Nazi sympathizer and hated Jews. Arthur Posnansky, on the other hand, was no follower of Hörbiger, but he did support the theory that Tiwanaku had been destroyed by flooding at the end of the last ice age. The oldest building phase in Tiwanaku, at least, is from before the last ice age. Edmund Kiss, on the other hand, was certainly a follower of Hörbiger—at least inasmuch as the World Ice Theory was concerned, I've never read anything about him being an antisemite. The next man in our list of researchers actually was a Jew: Prof. Hans Schindler Bellamy. In 1974, this highly educated and dear old man handed me a copy of his book with a personal dedication and begged me to make sure that researchers never turned their backs on Tiwanaku. I'm still doing that to this day.[61]

A Colossal Discovery

Archaeologists working under the patronage of the American Museum of Natural History in New York started excavations at Tiwanaku in 1932. Accompanying them, as a kind of coordinator, was Professor Arthur Posnansky. In the earth of the so-called "old temple" the Americans found a block of stone that they initially were unable to lift out. As they dug deeper they realized they had found a huge statue that had been worked from a single monolithic column. (See images 1.13 and 1.14.) The diggers estimated its weight to be around 20 tons. The block was made of reddish sandstone, and it was damp and covered in a mixture of dirt and clay soil. It must have been lying in its moist bed for thousands of years. Using beams and rope pulleys, they heaved the statue out of the mire and set it initially on a wooden plinth to dry.

A few weeks later, after they had gently scraped away the dirt with soft brushes, they discovered that the column was covered in fantastic messages. On its head it wore a hat, and on both sides of its long nose there were two rectangular eyes. The hands converging on the figure's chest were holding objects that look like cups. Underneath were two winged beings of the same kind as on the Gateway of the Sun. Finally, there were indefinable scales on the thighs and feet, each of which bears five toes. The diggers stared in amazement as they saw the rear

1.13.

The Great Idol during and after its excavation. Public domain images.

1.14.

side of this mighty form. It appeared to be a message from the ancient past! There were engraved faces, like those on the Gateway of the Sun, and to the right and left there were winged beings, crowns, scepters, snakes, condor heads, and so on. (See image 1.15.) The more than a thousand engravings are all aligned in perfect symmetry; not a 10th of a millimeter is free on either side. The master of engraving who committed his ideas to stone all those millennia ago must have used some sort of stencil; otherwise this work would just not have been possible. But what was the message he or they were trying to convey? What was it all supposed to show?

Arthur Posnansky deciphered the engravings as a calendar and promptly became a figure of scorn. One reason was that Posnansky's calendar stretched back more than 15,000 years into the past, which is something that could never be accepted by the "guild" of archaeology. As far as they were concerned, the oldest cultures belonged to the Egyptians and Sumerians, and certainly not some unknown South Americans. This was the same logic behind the criticism of the calendar variant on the Gateway of the Sun, as deciphered by Edmund Kiss. It was just not acceptable that any culture on the South American continent could be older than those of the Near East. If you thought that archaeo- and other-ologists didn't start getting in each other's hair until our times, then think again! You should read some of the polemic and ridicule being propagated in pamphlets between 1910 and 1945. Back then, as now, no trick was too low. The interpretations developed by Posnansky, Kiss, and others were subjected to academic scorn, without anyone taking the time to actually check out the facts. Kiss and Posnansky (and a number of later researchers) clearly showed the existence of the tidemark of a former major body of water on the Bolivian high plateau—it can still be seen today!—but this was ignored. Posnansky and Co. revealed the thick layer of bone-bearing sediments through which the Lake Titicaca railroad still runs today. That didn't interest any of the academic critics. Posnansky, and many after him, clearly demonstrated the glacial trails in Tiwanaku and the ruins that

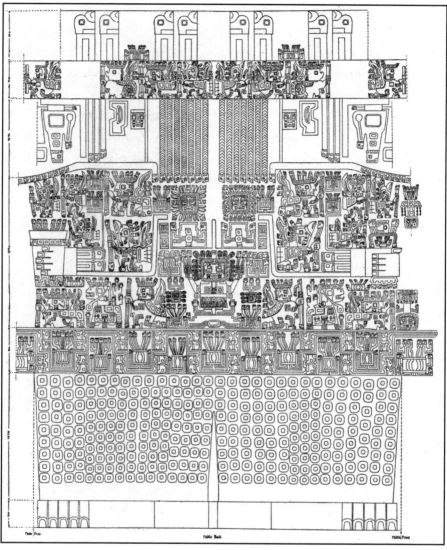

1.15. Detail of the unbelievably precise work on the back of the statue the "Great Idol." Public domain image.

lay under them. But who cares about that? (Any tourist who visits the Inca city of Cuzco in Peru can marvel at such "glacial chutes" next to the Inca fortress of Sacsayhuamán. *And they are not hundreds of thousands of years old*; otherwise they'd be just as weathered as the other rocks all around.)

Without exception, all of the geologists who examined Tiwanaku between 1900 and 1950 confirmed that the area—along with some of its ruins—must have stood underwater at some time. The residues show it too clearly. I can remember the great staircase well. It is covered in a layer of lime scale (calcium) that is so hard you need a knife to scratch it off. That didn't interest any of the critics who—and this is the greatest irony—never even visited the highlands. Back then, it was standard practice to fudge, lie, fake, and suppress—anything to avoid destroying the image of beatific archaeological evolution. Geological facts are ignored by archaeology when they don't fit into the establishment's rigid view of the world. It was so back then, and it often still is today.

Of course, Posnansky and Co. did make the odd mistake, and their interpretations of the calendar did sometimes stretch the imagination. Nevertheless, it can be clearly seen that Tiwanaku and Puma Punku could never in a million years fit in with a Stone Age culture. And it's easy enough to substantiate this claim.

After Posnansky's death, Professor Hans Schindler Bellamy and Dr. Paul Allen picked up the work on the engravings on the huge statue—commonly known as the Great Idol. This was already a few years after the Second World War. And again, the conclusion was that it was a kind of calendar. Professor Schindler Bellamy even believed that the engravings on the statue were older than those on the Gateway of the Sun. He presented tables and lists; every minute detail was calculated forward and backward; more than a thousand engravings were taken into account, and not a single one was ignored. It didn't change anything. The illustrations on the Great Idol still constituted the most phenomenal calendar imaginable, and the astronomical dates depicted on it reach back as far as 27,000 years before the birth of Christ.

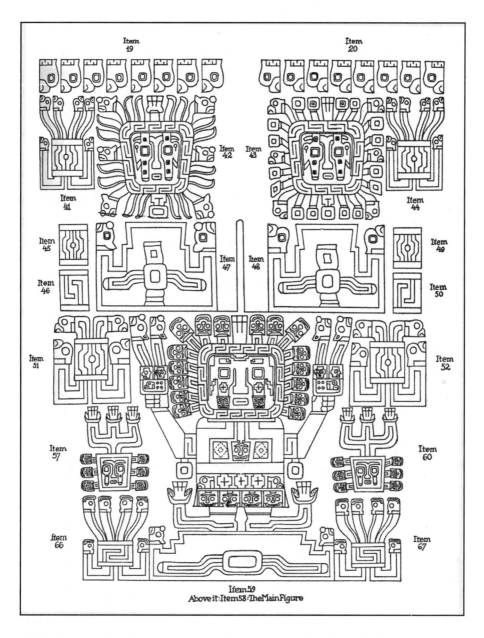

1.16. Excerpts from the calendar calculations by Dr. Hans Schindler Bellamy. Public domain image.

Professor Schindler Bellamy knew the problems that were likely to be stirred up with any dating that stretched that far back into the past. He knew of the ancient cultures of Egypt and Sumeria. Nevertheless, the engravings on the Great Idol show immutable periods. What could be done to solve this discrepancy? Professor Schindler Bellamy argued for a rise and fall of prehistoric cultures. There must have been, he argued, other high cultures before the Egyptian culture that had foundered and disappeared for whatever reasons. Unthinkable? Not really. After all, that is exactly what Plato reported two and a half millennia ago in his *Laws*. Back then he wrote of "earlier, frequent breakdowns of mankind caused by floods" from which "only a fragment of the human race was able to save itself."[62] Anyone who knows Plato's writings also knows that the concept of earlier civilizations—including of course Atlantis—apocalypses and new civilizations did not arise with Hans Hörbiger. This kind of lore is already thousands of years old.

Irrefutable Evidence

Curiously enough, it is not even necessary to squabble about Tiwanaku's age. And not necessary to pick sides regarding the calendar theories, glacier melts, or cosmic catastrophes. Why not? It's because there is one extremely solid and incontestable argument—a piece of proof that is inarguable and inerasable. It is a marvel, that not even the most hard-nosed critic could ignore.

Geologist Alphons Stübel took precise measurements from some of the stone blocks from Puma Punku during the 1870s. These highly exact, technical drawings still exist. They can be seen in Stübel and Uhle's book, *Die Ruinenstätte von Tiahuanaco im Hochland des alten Perú*. I present some of them here so you can see for yourself: the pieces are measured with extreme precision.

Take a close look!

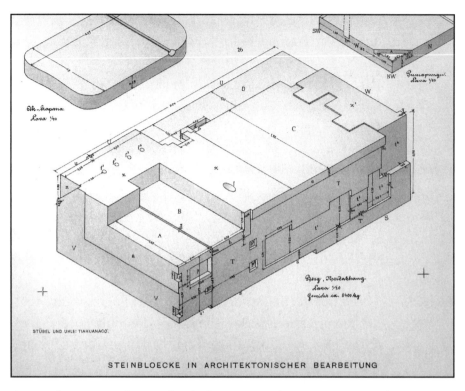

STEINBLOECKE IN ARCHITEKTONISCHER BEARBEITUNG

1.17. This picture shows a level of precision of measurement and workmanship that simply would not be possible with Stone Age tools. Public domain image.

Block 1:   It is rectangular: 9 feet long and 5.2 feet wide. The block has six main surfaces: top, bottom, and four sides. These six surfaces are subdivided into diverse smaller rectangular and quadratic planes. On the front—to the left in the picture—Alphons Stübel labeled one rectangle and two small squares with the letter "P." This is where any Stone Age tool—regardless of which one you care to choose—would just lie down and give up the ghost, even if you stretch your imagination a bit and add copper or iron tools to the mix, regardless of whether it's stone axes or chisels. Just try to re-create one of those precisely chiseled forms marked with a "P" in a piece of diorite—it's not possible! Another, even smaller, rectangle can be found on the surface of the block, on the left edge. Right next to it, you can see a slot or a groove. Some kind of object must have fit precisely into it. The same applies for the rear (right) side of the front side. This strip must have been the seat for a counterpart, just as must have been the case with countless other recesses. On top of all this, the block is a wedge shape. The back (the upper part of the sketch) is thicker than the front. All this adds up to planning. There's simply no way around it. Stübel calculated the weight of the block to be 18,500 pounds. The material is diorite—hardness grade 8.

Block 2: This is not the underside of block one. The size is different, but the precision work is the same. You only need to look at the cleanly cut protrusion on the lower front edge and the steps at the front and above left.

Blocks 3–5: This is an unbelievable feat of engineering, as some of the blocks fit perfectly into their counterparts. (Lift them up, turn them around, and stand them on their heads.) All that then remains is the upper part of the next "cross block," which then slots into the next piece. These are what are usually known in the construction trade as prefabricated elements—think of them as something like Lego blocks. Every groove and every recess were accurately calculated and precisely drawn. On coca or maize leaves? Skins? In the sand? Scratches in stone maybe? Or chords laid out on the ground? You can bet your bottom dollar they didn't just set off haphazardly with their chisels to create this precision work. There's just no way it would have been possible without precise architectural planning.

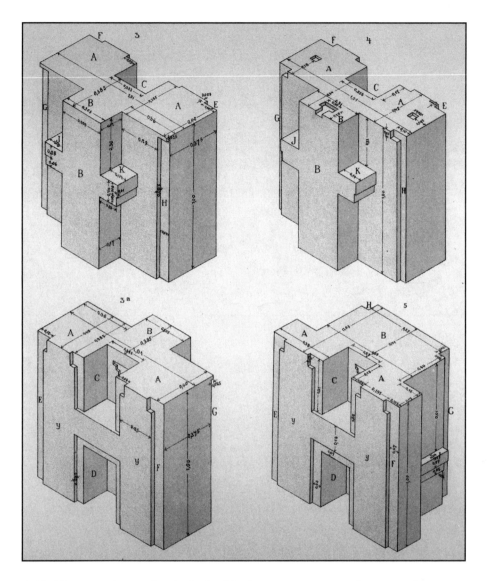

1.18. The precision with which the blocks were cut is simply astounding. Public domain image.

1.19. Could Stone Age craftsmen really have produced such levels of accuracy and consistency?

Without Tools or Plans?

Nowadays, work like this would be carried out using milling machines and high-speed precision drills—water or air cooled. And these tools would be guided by stainless steel templates. Let's not forget that we're talking about hard diorite here. That means the tools that were used must have been harder than the blocks that were being worked. Let's add to this the fact that they would have needed some kind of levers and cranes to lift the preprepared blocks and fit them into each other without any kind of accidents or damage taking place. These blocks fit into each other like safe doors—but with a whole variety of surfaces, rectangles, squares, and levels. Modern concrete elements are utterly primitive compared with the techniques used in Puma Punku. Closing your eyes or just looking the other way doesn't cut the mustard here. Holy Atahualpa help us! Which Stone Age geniuses do they expect us to believe in? This turns their comfortable evolution theory on its head! The gray-green diorite block, with its immaculate smooth finish and its utterly precise, perpendicularly milled groove, is enough to pull the pants down on this Stone Age fairy tale on its own—let alone the other pieces shown here.

Any claim or assertion is nothing more than an unproven assumption. But as far as Puma Punku is concerned, I'm not claiming anything—I'm talking hard facts. The Aymara, the pre-Incan tribe that allegedly created this masterpiece, cannot be responsible because:

- The Aymara were a Stone Age people. They could never have transported these heavyweight blocks almost 40 miles.

- The technology used here is way beyond anything that Stone Age man is known to have had at his disposal.

- The overall planning and the specifics are based on geometric measurements. High-level architectural skills have been used here.

- The builders would have needed to have known the exact stability or brittleness—in other words, the degree of hardness—of the material.

- The sheer number of architectural elements would have required a writing system or something equivalent. It's simply not possible to do something like this from memory, and it would have been beyond the planning capacity of our Stone Age geniuses. (These days we plan things like this on computers!)

Archaeologists talk of copper or lead brackets being used to hold the platforms together with a kind of carabiner fastening. This is because copper and lead casting have actually been found in Puma Punku. Heaven only knows why anyone at any time may have used lead or copper in Puma Punku, but it certainly can't have been simply as fastenings for these heavy platforms.

1.20. The slabs were originally held together with fastenings. Image courtesy of Tatjana Ingold, Solothurn, Switzerland.

Lead is a very soft metal, and in its pure form you can scratch it using just your fingernail. Its melting point is 621° Fahrenheit; its boiling point 3,182° Fahrenheit. Lead alloys would be possible, of course, but this assumes some kind of metallurgic expertise. Copper has a hardness grade of 3 (iron is 4.5). None of these soft metals would have been able to hold the incredibly heavy platforms in Puma Punku together. And certainly not when exposed to the kinds of temperature variations that are seen in Bolivia. As early as 1869, Johann Jakob Tschudi wondered:

> Even more than by the mere fact that they were actually able to move these blocks, we are astounded by the sheer technical brilliance of the masonry work, especially when one takes into account that the indigenous laborers possessed absolutely no iron tools and that the alloys of copper and tin they had were far too soft to work the granite. [Author's note: Tschudi was wrong in one respect, of course. No granite was used in Puma Punku; it was diorite, which is equally as hard.] How they accomplished this is a mystery. The most plausible view is that they achieved their final polish by rubbing the stone with a fine stone powder or some siliceous plants.[63]

1.21.   *1.22.*

High-level planning and core boring that did not exist during the Stone Age. Author's own images.

My dear, long-dead compatriot Tschudi: If they had used stone powder or siliceous plants, the workers in Puma Punku would not only have had to rub for hundreds of years to polish the huge stone slabs, but also would have needed precision instruments as the platforms all feature various planes and inclinations.

The Courage to Be Logical

Something's not quite right in Puma Punku, even if you leave aside Professor Posnansky's dating and ignore the calendars of Dr. Edmund Kiss and Professor Schindler Bellamy (and others!). The working of the stone is enough in itself.

Today, the calendar calculations made by Posnansky, Kiss, and Schindler Bellamy have all been discounted. The well-meaning talk is of academic errors. Hörbiger's World Ice Theory has been thrown out, today's moon is not repsonsible for the destruction of Tiwanaku, and there were no earlier high cultures. Basta! It's actually true that the Tiwanaku calendar could never be fit to our contemporary calendar—these days you would say the data are just not compatible. The industrious information collectors Posnansky, Kiss, and Schindler Bellamy all knew that. Their calendar had different months, days, and hours than ours. (Just as an aside: The Maya calendar system (see

Chapter 4) consists of a number of different calenders that mesh like cogwheels. Thus the "God Calendar"—also known as the "Tzolk'in"—consisted of 260 days. The 260-day calendar is, however, utterly useless for the seasons of the Earth. It's no good for sowing or harvesting, winter or spring. And yet it existed. So which planet was it good for?) As far as the Tiwanaku calendar is concerned, there remains one key question: Why is it, then, that despite this every single one of the more than one thousand tiny details on the statue the Great Idol corresponds with one another? As far as Edmund Kiss's year is concerned, we're talking about a year of 12 months at 24 days—except February and March with 25—and days with 30 hours of 22 minutes each. Well, the question can't be answered by looking at *our* calendar! Kiss's calculations don't fit to *our* calendar—but they certainly do fit to the other one. Who knows then with any certainty which calendar would have been valid before the last ice age? *We* deny the existence of any civilization before the last ice age—ergo the Tiwanaku calendar is wrong. And in the process, we blindly sweep the geological facts under the carpet. Are we not just making it too easy for ourselves?

The latest variation on the Tiwanaku calendar comes from Jorge Miranda-Luizaga, who at least is a Bolivian and knows both the culture and the language of his countrymen. He approaches the Tiwanaku calendar from the perspective of the Aymara, whose language he speaks fluently. The result is a practical calendar that repeats itself year for year and has its roots in the religious cultures of the Aymara.[64] Maybe Luizaga's solution is the only correct one; I can't say with any certainty. I *can* judge the technology, the planning, the transport, and the architectural draftsmanship that have been used to create the blocks in Puma Punku. And that certainly doesn't fit in with the former Aymara tribe. And this brings up another question that has been completely ignored in all of the literature on Tiwanaku: Why on earth did a Stone Age culture actually *need* such precisely calculated and perfectly smoothed blocks like those that can still be seen in Puma Punku?

For us, the term *Stone Age* refers generally to a people without metal tools. Stone Age is clearly a highly flexible concept, because the Stone Age is not an age in the sense that it fits in with any global calendar. Depending on geographical location, the Stone Age was 4000 BC or—among the South Sea folk—500 AD. In Brazil's Upper Amazon region there are still Stone Age tribes living today.

When a Stone Age people decide to erect a large building they somehow manage to drag, jockey, or tow the blocks to their chosen location and pile them up on top of each other using whatever methods are on hand. To make sure the walls don't collapse, they use pins and mortises—a kind of key and lock—that need to be chiseled or hollowed out. They never use the kind of engineering arts witnessed in Puma Punku. Are you getting the picture yet?

Even the carbon-14 datings of bones and wood fragments found in and around Tiwanaku are not exactly convincing. (C-14 is a method of dating that is based on measurements of the levels of radioactive carbon isotope C-14). The ruins and platforms could have been lying around for a very long time before later visitors used them to camp in or just came and pottered around. Today, it is *their* organic remains that are being dated. What good is that? (I know plenty more examples of this kind of thing.)

In our times, the established wisdom is that the Tiwanaku culture existed from around 300 BC until 1100 AD. You can forget Posnansky's 15,000 years. As you can also forget all the calendar variations, the silt layers, the bone sediment, or coastal markings. There have been a number of attempts at reconstruction.[65] But you can't really blame the archaeologist or architects if any attempt at reconstruction must remain little more than a patchwork. Too much material has been dragged off over the centuries, taken away and used to build streets and churches, broken down by the forces of nature, or simply been shot to pieces. Architects from the University of California, Berkeley, who have done sterling work in Tiwanaku and used computers for their reconstruction, were forced to admit: "The fragmentary remains are an insufficient basis from which to gain an understanding of the significance or meaning the architecture may have had for the people of Tiwanaku."[66]

Confronted with the precision work carried out by the creators of Tiwanaku/Puma Punku all those thousands of years ago, today's commentators can only talk of "fascinating compositions" and "incredibly tight fit[s],[...] deviating from each other by no more than a millimeter."[67]

We are the prisoners of our own way of thinking—and hanging constantly on the umbilical cord of evolution. For heaven's sake, please don't serve us up with anything so spectacular from ancient times! People like me, who ask questions on the basis of the platforms still around in Puma Punku today and the surveying techniques that can still be proven today, are considered eccentrics. Burn the heretics at the stake! And when that doesn't work, pour scorn on them! Hold them up to ridicule! As if I didn't actually already know all the literature in Tiwanaku and Puma Punku. Despite this, I allow myself the freedom to ask some legitimate questions.

New Answers

Legitimate questions? Too right!

In the summer of 1966, I shot some pictures that really revealed something fascinating. They show a series of monoliths and some individual free-standing monoliths. (See image 1.23 on page 81.) In this picture, the tops of five monoliths can be seen rising out of the ground. All of them display 90-degree recesses, which once would have served as anchor points for some kind of cross-blocks. At the top of the huge monolith you can see a clean, 90-degree cut. Another of the photos shows—as plain as the nose on your face—an extremely fine groove from top to bottom. When you compare this with today's reconstruction of the wall, there's no sign of recesses, right angles, or

1.23. Monoliths with 90-degree recesses (photo from 1966). Author's own image.

even a cleanly cut groove. The interstitial spaces have simply been filled in with stones. The former recesses and the groove, which after all were an intrinsic part of the monolith all those millennia ago and provide clues to whatever techniques were used, seem to have vanished into thin air. Is this just a case of "retouching"? It gets better.

The earlier water pipes—from which intact cornerpieces were found in the ground back in 1966—are now sitting at the top of the reconstructed wall. Later a sunken inner courtyard was re-created and heads were set into its walls that orginally had nothing to with this wall. The assiduous Bolivian and international reconstruction teams have put in a lot of effort to revive the former glory of Tiwanaku. Some of it has been reconstructed to death.

There is still one possibility for getting a little bit closer to solving the riddle of Puma Punku. Of course it is one that is harder to swallow than all the rest: Schliemann's route via the myths and legends.

- Viracocha, the god of "the flowing lava sea," is said to have been one of the helpful gods in Tiwanaku.
- The place was built "in a single night."
- This happened "long before the time of the Incas."
- Carried out by "unknown and powerful beings."
- All of this happened "before the flood."
- Akapana (the main temple) means "the place where the observers dwell" in the Aymara language.
- The original name of Puma Punku is said to be "Winay-Marca" (eternal city).
- The huge statue is called Pachamama (mother of the cosmos).

On the Gateway of the Sun the major god is depicted, flanked by 48 further winged figures.

I know—*not I believe!*—that our planet was visited by extraterrestrials before the Flood. I've written 25 books about it and, even if some of my evidence hasn't been so solid or even rebuttable, there are still too many things that are simply irrefutable. Anyone who has actually invested any significant amount of time examining the material will know I am right. The others should just take a moment to listen. Our forefathers lived in the Stone Age. They didn't understand anything and believed—erroneously, of course—that the ETs were gods. Those of us living today know that there are no gods; our forefathers didn't have this knowledge. These beings that were called gods back then have made their way into our myths and legends and even the major religions. In Enoch, Plato, and others this occurred—without any doubt—*before the Flood.*[68]

The visitors studied mankind, as today's ethnologists do, and occasionally gave out a few friendly tips to help the primitives on their way toward civilization. This can be proven. Just like mountaineers attempting to conquer mighty Everest, they needed the odd base camp here and there to store their technical equipment and protect it from the curiosity of mankind or from wild animals. So in one night, they built Puma Punku—the eternal city in the eyes of the indigenous people, the place where the observers dwell.

It's precisely here that the critics jump in with the observation that extraterrestrials would never use stone. They would be able to use other materials. Excuse me! When our astronauts finally get to building on the Moon and Mars, they'll use the raw materials that are on hand. They won't be dragging steel and other artificial materials to the next planet.

Our extraterrestrial visitors carried out their ethnological work; other groups may have exploited mineral resources; and a small number taught the more gifted among the indigenous folk about astronomy and other practical skills. Maybe just a little bit of development aid?

To take this contemporary interpretation a little further, the core of the original temple—here Puma Punku—was nothing more than a storehouse (base camp) for extraterrestrial technology. It may also have served as a school for a few of the more "switched on" and curious locals.

When they left, the ETs promised to return in the distant future. This idea became a firm component in mankind's religious thinking. Following the extraterrestrials' departure, some kind of natural catastrophe was visited upon the Earth—for whatever reason. The poor maltreated Earth recovered, and soon groups of people gathered in mute bewilderment in front of the mighty remains of the former base camp. "Once the gods lived here," they murmured. "They built this place in a single night. No man lifted a finger in help." In wonderment, they ran their fingers along the fine grooves in the diorite, the rectangular recesses, the polished slabs. The natives took word of what they had seen to the next valley. Soon, people from all around came to admire the gods' works, the "holy shrine" from which the gods spied on the people. Puma Punku became a place of pilgrimage. Soon the first temples were built to honor the gods. The people began to watch the heavens. After all, hadn't the gods said that they had come from the stars? Generations were born and died. Tiwanaku was built, one piece at a time.

It's a way of looking at events that at least explains the problem of the various different architectural styles and the "know-how" from diverse epochs.

I beg you to also consider the "god variant" in your observations of Puma Punku. It solves a number of problems and cannot simply be ignored just because it comes from me. After all, one thing is certain: The technology used here had nothing to do with any Stone Age race.

So what do we do now? Dig! Even today. That's just what is happening, thanks to a group called Akakor Geographical Exploring. With support from Bolivia's Ministry of Culture and archaeologists from the UNAR (Unidad Nacional de Arqueología), its researchers managed to discover artificially built shafts and water pipes underneath the so-called Pyramid of Tiwanaku. Monolithic slabs—highly polished and precisely worked like all the rest—make up the side walls and the ceiling of these subterranean passageways. In some places, the seals of the great stone slabs were no longer completely intact, and over the millennia 15-centimeter-long stalactites had formed. In several places, the team found damage that had clearly been caused by seismic disturbances.

Nobody knows what these tunnels and shafts under Tiwanaku and Puma Punku were used for. Posnansky was already writing about them in 1913! And Kiss in 1939! Yet they were simply laughed at by the oh-so-serious scientific community of the time. So, what now? I'm still waiting for the "sensible" answer from those establishment dolts whose heads are eternally stuck in yesterday that the Stone Age schmucks probably needed these megalithic tunnels so that they could play marbles in the dark.

There is yet another mystery that can easily checked by anyone at anytime—by laymen as well as experts: As early as 1968, I had noticed strange anomalies on my pocket compass. Sometimes the needle changed direction completely within two blocks. I demonstrated this strange phenomenon to several groups of passing tourists. In the meantime, my colleague Hartwig Hausdorf has made more precise measurements.[69] In one of the stone blocks in Puma Punku there are five depressions—one over the other. Hausdorf passed a compass of these holes and registered a magnetic deviation from hole to hole. It goes like this: the first hole had a deviation of 5 degrees, the second hole had a deviation of 10 degrees, the third hole had a deviation of 20 degrees, the fourth hole had a deviation of 40 degrees, and the fifth hole had a deviation of 80 degrees! He repeated the experiment several times in front of astonished witness.

A physicist would question an anomaly like this; an archaeologist doesn't know anything about it.

CHAPTER 2

NOTHING NEW UNDER THE SUN

Stem cells, those mysterious microscopic monsters, are again the subject of front-page headlines these days. The reason for all this excitement is a decision by the British parliament: Great Britain is allowing the culturing of hybrids or chimeras consisting of human and animal genetic material.

Many politicians are still fuming about this, claiming that as far as bioethics is concerned Britain is "walking an ever more dangerous path."[1] Many scientists, though, such as John Burn, a professor at the University of Newcastle, think the new law on embryos is completely alright: "A cell cannot have a soul," he maintains.[2]

What are these geneticists actually up to? Are they playing God in their dubious laboratories?

Breeding is nothing new. We've been doing it with fruit trees, for instance, since time immemorial. Certain attributes from one tree are transferred to another tree by means of "grafting." In this way, genetic characteristics pass from one tree to another—without any need for people to interfere in the process. This kind of cultivation of trees, flowers, or cereals is part of everyday life, and nobody raises an eyebrow over it. Where's the difference between cultivation and genetics?

In genetics, nuclear material is artificially removed from one cell and implanted in the cell of another being that has previously had its nucleus removed. This was how the famous sheep Dolly was bred in 1997. She was a 100-percent copy of the donor animal. This process is called cloning and always involves cells from the same kind of animal. (Since then, Dolly has had her own, healthy young.)

Chimeras or hybrids, however, are created from different species, such as human beings and cows—as is indeed the case in Britain. The nuclei are removed from one human cell and one bovine cell. Then the human nucleus is implanted in the empty bovine cell. A short electrical impulse is used to stimulate cell division, and thus the human genetic information is multiplied manifold.

Madness? It happens in nature all the time—without any intervention from mankind. So-called "retroviruses," such as the AIDS virus, bore into cells and then copy their own genetic information into the DNA of the host. This cell reproduces and produces more AIDS virus cells. No geneticists are involved at all.

Why would scientists want to cross humans with cows? Have they lost their marbles? Surely, any basic research has some kind of long-term objective. Indeed, this is the case here. Geneticists hope that—sometime in the future—they will be able to manipulate genetic information in such a way that conditions such as Alzheimer's disease or multiple sclerosis will be eliminated forever. It's sometimes called "therapeutic cloning," and it is a science that is still in its infancy. But to advance their knowledge, the geneticists require cells, and up until now they have been using egg cells from young women. This has inevitably engendered political and religious problems, because this "practice material" is, after all, human. The egg cells from cows, on the other hand, are available in the billions from the slaughterhouses. The combination of man and cow has nothing to do with Frankenstein, however. It is not about creating talking cows or mooing bipeds. Why not?

Cells multiply into ever larger clumps. Before these can ever develop into an actual being, they need to be implanted into a uterus, and that is still strictly forbidden. But what happens if it is done in secret? British law requires that hybrid human-bovine embryos are destroyed after 14 days. What's more, the probability that any of these kinds of cell clumps live any longer than that is extremely remote—but not impossible. It depends on the biotechnological technologies used at a particular laboratory.

Outside of Great Britain, all sorts of even more outrageous things have been going on. Australian geneticists working on biologist Andrew Pask's team at the University of Melbourne managed to transplant the genetic material of a Tasmanian tiger into a mouse embryo and successfully managed to get the cells to multiply. The alarming thing about it is that the Tasmanian tiger has actually been extinct for many decades and the cellular material they used had been lying around in a jar of alcohol for at least 100 years! Professor Pask wasted no time in announcing that by using his technique it would even be possible to bring animals like dinosaurs back to life as long as they could scrape together enough DNA (deoxyribonucleic acid). And it would be no problem at all to produce a Neanderthal man.[3] Similar experiments are going in labs all over the world. In London there is even a "DNA bank" storing the basic genetic material of all kinds of animals.

Memories of the Future

Strangely enough, I discussed all of these things that are now the object of extensive research in my book *Chariots of the Gods* 40 years ago.[4] Here's a quote from that book:

> And whence came the first audacious idea that the cells of the body had to be preserved so that the corpse, preserved in a very secure place, could be awakened to new life after thousands of years?... Did space travelers in prehistory already possess knowledge that we must gain anew? Did unknown intelligences already know the methods with which to treat bodies so that they could be revived in so many thousand years?[5]

Nowadays, the field of genetics is actually realizing the science-fiction idea of *Jurassic Park*!

What is being tried today—and will someday succeed—was already being done thousands of years ago. And there are ancient witnesses: Manetho is the name of one of them. He was a scribe in the holy temples of Egypt. The Greek historian Plutarch mentioned Manetho as one of the contemporaries of the first Ptolemaic kings (304–282 BC).[6] Manetho wrote his three-volume work in Sebennytos, a city on the Nile Delta. The second witness, Eusebius (who died in 339 AD), is another classic historian. He is recorded in church annals as the Bishop of Caesarea and in his magnum opus, *Chronographia,* he quoted many ancient sources, which he deliberately and meticulously recorded. Manetho and Eusebius complement each other in their descriptions of the ancient records. Manetho begins his history by listing the names of the gods and demigods, and even quotes the years of their dominion—citing spans that would have most archaeologists in paroxysms. The gods of Egypt, he asserts, ruled for 13,900 years, and the demigods that followed them for another 11,000 years.[7] The gods, Manetho wrote, created various beings: monsters and chimeras of all kinds. Eusebius confirmed exactly the same thing. The following quote from ancient sources fits in incredibly well with the contemporary debate on these hybrids:

> ...In those times, the gods created monstrous beasts with strange appearances. There were men with two wings, and some with four wings and two faces. They had one body, but two heads, of a man and a woman, and two sets of genitals, male and female. Other men had the legs and horns of a goat, or the hooves of a horse, or the rear end of a horse and the front of a man.... Other beasts they made, such as bulls with human heads; dogs with four bodies and fish tails protruding from their rear end; horses with dogs' heads...and other monsters with the head and body of a horse, but the tail of a fish; and other beasts with the form of all kinds of wild animals. As well as these [beasts], there were fish and reptiles and snakes and many other strange creatures, each of which had a different appearance. Representations of them were set up in the temple of Belus.[8]

It's pretty strong stuff that Eusebius serves up from the ancient sources. Men with wings? Is this nothing but old nonsense? If so, why are there so many reliefs depicting just this on columns and sculptures in all the major museums of the world? In the world of archaeology they even have a name for them. They call them "winged geniuses."

2.1.

Winged geniuses working by the tree of life. Author's own images.

2.2.

2.3.

*Hybrid
creatures on
a Sumerian
cylinder seal.
Author's own
images.*

2.4.

2.5.

Men with the "the legs and horns of a goat"—utter claptrap? How about taking a look at some Sumerian and Babylonian cylinder seals? (See images 2.3, 2.4, and 2.5.) They feature images of these chimeras in their hundreds. And men with the "the hooves of a horse" and the "rear end of a horse and the front of a man"—did they exist, too? Say hello to the centaur! And the gods created "bulls with human heads"? Holy Apis in Egypt help us! Including the Minotaur of Crete!

Monsters From the Past

The past steamrolls the future. Up until now, all these chimeras have been explained away in psychological terms—wishful thinking, reveries, and mythology. So, what is a sphinx? Simple, it's a hybrid. Of course, if you mention the word *sphinx* then everyone immediately thinks of the huge lion figure with the human head next to the Great Pyramid of Gizeh. But sphinges (yes, that's the plural of sphinx) come

2.6. A sphinx in Luxor. Author's own image.

in all shapes and sizes: lions' bodies with rams' heads, dogs' or goats' bodies with human heads, rams' bodies with birds' heads, human bodies with birds' heads, and so on and so on! There are whole avenues lined with all kinds of sphinges in among the desert sand. Anyone who has whiled away a few hours in a large museum or browsed through a book about Sumer, Assur, and Egypt will be able to sing the song of songs about these "strange creatures," as Eusebius calls them.

On the Black Obelisk of Shalmaneser III, now kept in the British Museum, two men can be seen leading strange beings with human heads and animal bodies on short leashes—monkeys, the experts would have us believe, but they are certainly not that. Two other hybrids can be seen being led on chains. One of these chimeras seems to be sucking on its thumb, and the other almost looks a bit to be

2.7. Hybrids on the Black Obelisk of Shalmaneser. Author's own image.

thumbing its nose at the man in front. These monsters are alive; that can be seen from the short leashes and chains. The picture speaks for itself! The accompanying cuneiform writing speaks of "captive human animals" that are to be offered up as sacrifices.

In the subterranean caverns of far off Ecuador in South America, there lies not only a metal library,[9] but also a collection of hybrid creatures, at least according to the eyewitness report of one Petronio Jaramillo Abarca:

> Moving to a third chamber, imagine my surprise to discover figures half human half animal as if all the mythologies had united to display themselves in gold and precious stones.... There were bodies with heads of hawks, with horses' feet, with wings; birds with human arms and legs...donkeys with faces of men. A multitude of combinations of beast and human....[10]

And some of these creatures, at least, are supposed to have really lived? Created by the gods? What on earth for? What use could these ominous gods possibly have had for these strange crossbreeds?

That the gods of the mythologies, the involuntary founding fathers of the major religions, were in fact visitors from distant galaxies is something I don't want to get into here. After all, I've written 25 books on the subject. The point is this: Any space-traveling species would be sure to know a whole host of other planets apart from the Earth. There would be worlds where it is hotter or colder than it is here, and yet other planets where the gravity would be greater or, alternatively, less strong. Take the Moon, for example, where we humans can make huge jumps of several yards. On Jupiter, on the other hand, we would be squashed flat by the extreme gravity.

The extraterrestrials would be sure to know all this. On the Earth, maybe they observed a scaled monster as it dozed by the Nile, seemingly unaffected by the blistering heat. We're talking, of course, about the mighty crocodile. Then they might observe the graceful might with which a lion devours a gazelle. So the aliens look at each other and wonder: What would happen if we combined the scaly armor of the crocodile with the bones and musculature of the lion to create a new life form, possibly to be used on a planet with different conditions to Earth? Thus the creation of the chimeras began. The extraterrestrials were probably only 30 or 40 years ahead of today's geneticists. Enough to decode the DNA and rearrange the building blocks of the genetic code.

The gods look on their creations with pride—while mankind looks on in fear. But then comes the point when the strangers must return to their mothership. It would, of course, be totally unnecessary and impractical for them to actually transport their artificially created monstrosities by spaceship. The extraterrestrials didn't need to take the actual chimeras with them. All they needed were a few samples of intact genetic information. That wouldn't be at all heavy, but would be enough for them to genetically engineer the creatures on a suitable planet. Ideally adapted to the local environment.

How can one back up a hypothesis like this?

Apis and Other Chimeras

First, there are a number of indications that can be found again and again: Ancient historians such as Manetho, Plutarch, Strabon, Plato, Tacitus, Diodorus, Herodotus, and the later church prelate Eusebius all wrote about it. Manetho reported that the artisans and masons had depicted these creatures in paintings and sculptures. That's right. There are thousands of them! We are also more than well aware of the god cults of the ancient races. The gods climbed into their "barques" and "winged sun disks" (Egypt); rode "heavenly pearls" (Tibet), "flying sea-shells" (the Maoris), "vimanas" (India), or—as described in the Old Testament—the "Lord's flaming chariot"; and came down to the people of the Earth. Added to this, you have the technological legacies, such as the incredibly accurately worked stones in Puma Punku. Finally, there is the fact that the gods also taught elements of their wisdom to mankind. There was a definite flow of information. The most eloquent descriptions of this can be found in the book of the antediluvian prophet Enoch.[11] Some random natural catastrophe—as the establishment is always trying to palm off on us—is certainly not the cause of *that*. They don't talk and certainly don't dictate their knowledge to willing listeners.

Extraterrestrials, worshiped and feared as gods by Stone Age peoples, were masters of the high art of genetics, and they used this knowledge on the Earth. What was their motivation? To create beings suitable for other planets.

Back in Egypt, there lived a holy monster, the Apis bull. The ancient Egyptians saw Apis as the offspring of the cosmos, a creation of the god Ptah. This earliest veneration is documented in depictions featuring star-bejeweled bull heads that were found near Abydos. Greek historian Plutarch (born around 50 AD) wrote that the divine animal was not born in a natural way, but rather was created by a beam that fell from the heavens.[12] Herodotus, too, noted that Apis was conceived via a "light from heaven."[13] Beneath the desert sands, in the so-called Serapeum, August Mariette found a stela dedicated to Apis. On it was written: "You have no father: you are born of the heavens."[14] Not only that, Apis also bore certain characteristics that set him apart from other bulls. Herodotus again: "The Apis bears distinctive marks: it is black with a white diamond on its forehead, the image of an eagle on its back, the hairs on its tail [are] double and [there is] a scarab under its tongue."[15]

Alongside Apis there were a number of other bulls, which, however, did not merit the same high status as Apis himself. And where are the mummies of the holy Apis?

On September 5, 1852, exuberant Frenchman August Mariette— who later founded the Egyptian Museum—found himself in a subterranean corridor in Saqqara. In the dust on the floor he discovered footprints, which must have been left by the priests thousands of years earlier. In front of him were two mighty sarcophagi. With great effort, the 40-ton lid of the sarcophagus was removed with crowbars and pulleys. Mariette wrote: "Thus I was certain that an Apis mummy must lay before me.... My first great concern was the head of the bull, but I found none. Within the sarcophagus lay a bituminous, stinking mass which crumbled at the slightest touch...in the midst of this confusion lay small bones and fifteen randomly positioned figurines...."[16]

Mariette discovered the same when he opened the second sarcophagus: "No skull, no large bones at all. Quite the contrary, an even greater multitude of tiny bone fragments."[17]

British explorer Sir Robert Mond, who excavated the so-called "Bucheum" (a burial chamber in the rocks under the temple ruins of Hermonthis), came to the same shattering conclusion. The sarcophagi contained either nothing or simply bitumen filled with bone fragments. In one sarcophagus, instead of the expected mummified bull, they found the mixed bones of jackals and dogs.[18]

In the catacombs of Abusir, Mond, this time accompanied by two Frenchmen, discovered further sarcophagi which they were sure would contain mummified bulls as these mighty granite containers actually contained bulls' heads with horns. At last! Carefully the French specialists, Monsieur Lortet and Monsieur Gaillard, cut open the millennia-old cords and gently pulled off one layer after another of linen. Their amazement was indescribable. Within they found a mixture of the bones of all kinds of animals, and for some of them they could not even identify the species. The second sarcophagus, a little more than 8 feet long and 3 feet wide, contained a motley mix of seven different animals. Here too they were unable to identify the species of two of the bones.

Religion Vs. Chopped-Up Bones

The ancient Egyptians didn't just mummify people; they mummified all kinds of animals as well: dogs, cats, crocodiles, birds, fish—everything. They did this—and any Egyptologist will confirm this—because they believed in rebirth. In order to be reborn, the body must be preserved. Anything else would be a sacrilege, blasphemy. As Sir Robert Mond opined: "The burial of a royal mummy in any but complete form would have been unthinkable in Egypt."[19]

So why the chopped-up bones?

The giant sarcophagi in the Serapeum beneath Saqqara are made of Aswan granite. Aswan is nearly 600 miles away from Saqqara. Just imagine the effort that that must have cost. Beneath Saqqara, miles of passages with side compartments were hewn from the rock. Hundreds of miles away in Aswan, specialists were blasting the hardest granite known in Egypt from the rock face, using methods that remain unknown. Subsequently, these rocky heavyweights had to be transported about 600 miles along the Nile, which back then involved navigating three sets of rapids. (Ships today have the advantage of using the locks.) After reaching Saqqara, these stone monstrosities were smoothed and polished in an unbelievably professional manner. The pictures prove it. Each one of these sarcophagi weighs between 60 and 100 tons! Strong arms with levers and rollers jockeyed these huge containers—carved from a single block of stone—into the pre-prepared tunnels and niches. They could not be lowered down from above, as the tunnels have a solid stone roof. So why did they go to all this effort?

Just to bury some chopped-up bones? And then pour greasy tar all over them and cover them up with a 40-ton lid? Their motivation must have been something other than pure faith in reincarnation—because in that case they *wouldn't have destroyed the body.*

So what have we got left?

Were the coffins plundered by grave robbers? Did monks smash up the contents of the sarcophagi? Well, the grave robber theory wouldn't explain why there are bone fragments from so many different animals in the sarcophagi. That it was god-fearing monks seems more likely. They could have smashed up the contents with heavy iron bars. But this explanation isn't very plausible either. If monks had been involved, then the traces of their destructive Christian wrath would be apparent: Bandages would be ripped up; idols would be smashed or melted down.

What did Auguste Mariette write after opening the sarcophagi? "Within the stinking mass lay a number of small bones, clearly already broken at the time of burial."[20] How is it that archaeologist Sir Robert Mond discover bones that he assumed to be "those of a jackal or dog"? I could hardly blame any anthropologist who didn't further examine bones that he had found under these circumstances. And how did anyone come up with the absurd idea of four-bodied dogs (Eusebius) with "fish tails protruding from their rear end"?

Dr. Ange-Pierre Leca is a doctor and a specialist for Egyptian mummies. He wrote about one sarcophagus containing "wonderfully bandaged bulls" that was discovered in the catacombs of Abusir: "...again it seemed to be just one single bull, but again we found the bones of seven animals...including one huge old bull. A third animal must have had two skulls."[21]

Excuse me? *Two skulls?* Let's return to our old friend Eusebius: "Many other strange creatures, each of which had a different appearance... one body but two heads."[22]

What seems so absurd—and made no sense at all to the Egyptologists, who knew that mummies were never destroyed because that would ruin any chance of reincarnation—seems to make sense from a contemporary perspective.

The gods had moved on, but they had left some of their chimeras behind. If these creatures were reborn, would they not continue to spread fear and consternation among the people of the future? This problem occupied the minds of the ancient priests—until suddenly they saw a way out of the mess. As long as the beasts remained alive, they were treated with awe and respect, prayed to and treated as divine. After their natural deaths, on the other hand, the bones of these unearthly creatures were smashed into tiny pieces and covered in tar. Sarcophagi were made of the hardest granite—so weighty and strong that no reborn monster could ever break its way out of the tomb. The mighty sarcophagi were not there to serve the process of reincarnation—rather the opposite: They were prisons for eternity.

Is it possible to prove this?

Just a few bones with intact DNA would be enough and our clever geneticists would soon be able to say if they were looking at DNA that has arisen through natural evolution or whether it was a targeted artificial mutation. Nowadays, any interference in the genome can be verified. Maybe analyses such as these have already taken place and have been classified as top secret. The god shock would just be too much for mankind to cope with. Because evidence of chimeras in the dim and distant past would be indisputable evidence of alien intervention. Why?

Because our forefathers all those thousands of years ago didn't have a clue about genetics. Because the ancient texts and the illustrations tell us so. And because the ETs had a compelling motive for doing it: the creation of specially adapted life forms for other planets.

I call it memories of the future.

CHAPTER 3

SCIENTIFIC? SCIENTIFIC!

"There are no absolute truths, and if there were, they would be boring."

—Theodor Fontane, 1819–1898

This sentence cannot really be applied to the exact sciences. Two plus two always makes four. And in geometry, A squared plus B squared always equals C squared. It may be boring, but "exact science" does indeed bring us many "absolute truths." Alongside all the many errors that are constantly being corrected.

However, our power of reason is not just impressed by the results gleaned by the exact sciences; the humanities—and these include so much that requires interpretation—violate our way of thinking no less. Religions fall into this category, as do philosophy, ethnology, and archaeology. Excuse me? Isn't archaeology a combined science that cites only verified findings?

Of course. But the findings still have to be interpreted. They are still the subject of interpretation. This interpretation, on other hand, relies on rationality—the zeitgeist—and, of course, on written historical evidence. Is that clear? Now here's a short extract from Popol Vuh, the greatest writing from the legacy of the K'iche' Maya.[1] It was composed or written an unknown amount of time ago in the highlands of what is now Guatemala.

> "Tepew Q'ukumatz
> E Alom, E K'ajplom,
> K'o pa ja'. Saqtetoj e k'o wi.
> E muqutal pa q' ug,
> Pa raxon...."

It might sound like Chinese to us, but to an expert it makes perfect sense. The text describes how the lord "Quetzal serpent" fathered children, descended from the heavens surrounded by light and covered in the feathers of the quetzal bird (hence the name). The quetzal serpent is said to have come from the blackness of the heavens, and so on. On the rear side of the folio 24 you can read how the gods first had to enter a "house of darkness" and needed torches. Consequently, they smoked cigars. (The god "Smoking Mirror" is depicted in numerous Maya temples.)

3.1.

The "smoking gods" in the Madrid Codex. Author's own images.

3.2.

I admire the Maya specialists who can read and translate the ancient language of the K'iche' Maya. Their skill is the result of the decades of hard work and the laborious efforts of the ethnologists who put together all the little pieces of the jigsaw. At the end of the day, though, these praiseworthy translations still remain subject to a great degree of interpretation in many respects. What do I mean? Interpretation is all down to the zeitgeist, the leading trend in "rational" thinking. And that is very flexible.

A "feathered snake" never existed. So in Guatemala, the quetzal bird seems a logical choice. It has an impressive plumage and may have even reminded the K'iche' Maya of a flying serpent. But the quetzal bird does not engender human children. Nor does it smoke! The Maya god "Smoking Mirror" also doesn't look anything like a quetzal bird in any shape or form.

A modern interpretation leaves room for a number of different possibilities, especially when contemporary viewpoints are brought together with other texts from other parts of the world. Impossible? Well, for the Maya specialists, just like the Egyptologists, text comparisons between Central America and Egypt are pretty much unthinkable. We're talking about two completely different cultures, they argue. That's right. So why is it, then, that when you start comparing the texts you keep finding all sorts of similarities? The "creation" in Popol Vuh is very similar to that in the first Book of Moses (Genesis). And there's more: If you read the Bible, you will discover that once the whole world "was of one language" (before the building of the Tower of Babel, that is). And it's no different in Popol Vuh. In the second book of Moses (Exodus) we find out how Moses held his staff out over the waters and divided them. The Maya tell the same story! Or in chapter 9, verse 17 of Genesis: "This is the token of the covenant, which I have established between me and all flesh that is on the earth...." And in Popol Vuh? "That will help you when you call me. It is the sign of our agreement...." And so on! Who was copying from whom? The authors of Popol Vuh couldn't have known anything about that Bible because their texts existed a long time before the Christian Spaniards arrived. So we can be pretty sure that there was no copying involved. These texts came about around the same campfire, so to speak.

Nowadays, in our times of worldwide networking and almost unlimited globalization, you would have thought that comparing texts would be the order of the day. But neither side wants to hear anything of it. The Maya archaeologist is a specialist in his own area; the Egyptologist in his. Without exception, a bunch of well-educated, well-integrated, and respectable researchers. The only problem is: they don't work together. Each group remains staunchily anchored by his own island of specialist isolation. Contemporary?

Pyramid Texts

In distant Egypt you will find the pyramid texts. What are they? They are engravings from the 5th and 6th dynasties—although it remains unclear how long the texts existed before they were chiseled into the granite. The pyramid texts are subdivided into "Utterances." These Utterances are overflowing with gods, who descend from the heavens to Earth, and pharaohs, who were granted the honor of visiting the world of the gods. Because our confused zeitgeist doesn't recognize any reality behind these stories, they are interpreted as being the wishful thinking of the priests or the journeys of the pharaohs after their deaths. Here are a few examples:[2]

(Utterance 511):	"Nut shouts for joy when I ascend to the sky. The sky thunders for me, the Earth quakes for me, the hail storm is burst apart and I roar as does Seth...."
(Utterance 267):	"A stairway to the sky is set up for me, that I may ascend on it to the sky; and I ascend on the smoke of the great censing. I fly up as a

bird and alight as a beetle on the empty throne which is in thy barque, O Re...that I may sit in your place and row over the heaven in your barque, O Re. That I may push off from the land in thy boat...."

(Utterance 302):   "The sky is clear, Sothis lives...the Two Enneads have cleansed themselves for me in Ursa Major [constellation].... My house in the sky will not perish, my throne on Earth will not be destroyed...."

(Utterance 482 C):   "May I fly up to heaven like the great star in the middle of the east...."

(Utterance 434):   "You have taken to yourself every god who possesses his barque that you may install them in the starry sky...."

(Utterance 472):   "The sky quivers, the Earth shakes before me. For I am a magician. I have come that I may glorify Orion...."

(Utterance 480):   "How lovely to behold when this god ascends into the sky, just as Atum, the father of the king, ascends to the sky...."

(Utterance 482):   "You must ascend to the heaven...your son Horus will accompany you to the starry sky; heaven is yours, the Earth is yours...."

(Utterance 553 + 563):   "The gates of heaven are open for you; the gates of the firmament are open for you...."

(Utterance 584):   "The doors of (?), which are in the firmament, are opened for me...lie open for me...."

(Utterance 669):   "The prince descends in a great storm from within the horizon...."

It goes on for pages like this. Heavenly portals are opened; gods descend in smoke and flames; pharaohs are allowed to fly with them; there are thunder and lightning all over the place; sand is thrown up into the air. Who is always behind it all? The gods. Whether it's in old India, in Tibet, in Japan, in the Bible (Ezekiel), or the Maya. *Now look here,* preach the Egyptologists: *These texts are not be compared with any kind of reality. They are about the ascensions of deceased pharaohs.* Well, somehow I doubt that. Looking at it from a modern perspective allows some quite reasonable and totally different conclusions, and there's nothing "anti-scientific" about them. Why don't the universities at least teach their students about the interconnections that are actually there? They could point out that a word like *heaven* does not necessarily have anything to do with a place of bliss and beatitude, and just as little to do with life after death. "Heaven" is also space—especially when it's mentioned in the same breath as attributes such as smoke, fire, quaking, noise, stars, and so on. What's unscientific about that? As long as the texts from each individual culture continue to be treated in isolation, then new insights will continue to be impossible.

In 1975, respected philosopher of science Paul Feyerabend, who taught for three decades in the University of California, Berkeley, announced his "anything goes" approach. It's another way of saying that anything is possible. The scientific world reacted with horror because "anything goes" or "anything is allowed" was a contradiction to the long-held belief in a continual scientific process of establishing the truth. Feyerabend postulated, however, that the results of any scientific method are limited by the methods themselves.[3] Indeed, many scientific innovations thrive not because methodological rules have been followed, but because they have been *broken.* Feyerabend was right, and his "anything goes" does not contradict scientific progress at all. So a comparison between the mythologies of ancient Egypt and Central America may go against the academic grain, but it does bring new answers and therefore the desired insights. Breaking the rules means eating from someone else's bowl—but only when there's a good reason for it. And there's plenty of them!

Divine Intervention

Spanning the gap between Egypt and Central America makes a whole lot of sense. In both places flaming gods rise into the heavens, even though—from the point of view of the archaeologists—the two cultures existed at different times. But who can say with absolute certainty where the origins of these cultures lay and whether there really were any transatlantic connections all those thousands of years ago. In the Museum of Leyden in Holland, you can see a jade tablet known in the scientific literature as the Leyden Plate. It was found in the Maya city of Tikal (now Guatemala). Following the tricky-to-translate name of a god, it reads: "the lords of the heavenly family of Tikal descended." Regardless of whoever these heavenly rulers may have been, it was really no different in ancient Egypt (or in China, Japan, Tibet, or India, come to mention it).

3.3. Winged sun disk, Karnak. Image courtesy of Tatjana Ingold, Sotothurn, Switzerland.

Visitors to the land on the Nile will be confronted by the so-called "winged sun disk" in practically every temple. It's a golden disk or bowl shape with colored, broadly spreading wings. Entire temple roofs (Dendera!) and countless temple entrances (Karnak!) are decorated with them. (See image 3.3 on page 113.) These winged sun disks are usually associated with the god Horus—the son of Osiris and Isis—whose seat was in the huge temple complex of Edfu (between Aswan and Luxor).

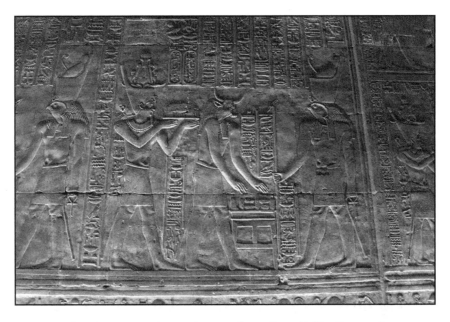

3.4. Osiris and Horus texts on the temple walls at Edfu. Image courtesy of Tatjana Ingold, Solothurn, Switzerland.

This is where the story of the winged sun disk is immortalized on one of Edfu's temple walls. The inscriptions describe how the god Ra and his retinue landed "in the west of this area, to the east of the Pechennu canal." His earthly representative, the pharaoh, was clearly in some sort of trouble, as he asked the heavenly flier to help him deal with his enemies:

The holy majesty Ra-Harmachis spoke to your holy person Hor-Hut: O you sun child, you exalted one, who is created by me, strike down the enemy that is before you without delay. Then Hor-Hut flew up to the sun in a great sun disk with wings upon it...when he viewed the enemies from the high heavens...he stormed down so violently upon them that they neither saw with their eyes nor heard with their ears. Within a short time not a head of them still stood living. Hor-Hut, shining and many-colored, returned in his form as a great winged sun disk to the ship of Ra-Harmachis.[4]

This text was translated in 1870. In other words, at a time when no Egyptologist would have known about supersonic flight. They didn't even have aircraft back then. But the attack described here definitely came from above (*"when he viewed the enemies from the high heavens"*) and it must have taken place at supersonic speeds (*"that they neither saw with their eyes nor heard with their ears"*). The results down here on Earth were correspondingly gruesome: *"Within a short time not a head of them still stood living."* The gods alone know what dreadful weapon they used against this Stone Age folk.

Whether Egypt, Central America, or anywhere else, all of these ancient texts are fed to us these days in a kind of psychological mush. This is a shame because interpretations are possible in every color of the rainbow. I find it hard just to imagine the "Saga of the winged sun disk" in an abstract way, flying blind as I am in the fog of religious/psychological dogma. After the god Ra-Harmachis had helped the pharaoh defeat his enemies, he succinctly notes: *"Here it is a pleasant place to live."* Afterward the surrounding lands are given a special name and the gods of heaven and Earth are praised. I suggest that maybe we shouldn't spend so much time reading about how other people think things are meant and the way we should, in their exalted opinions, see things, and instead look at the uncommented original texts.

"Hor-Hut flew up towards the sun as a great winged disk. Thus he has been known since as the Lord of Heaven...."[5] Lord of Heaven? What about something else? What about "space man"?

As the inscriptions from Edfu show, the divine assistance was the actual reason for the worship and popularization of the winged sun disk and not, as some would have us believe, the sun in some imaginary under- and overworld. The Edfu text says it clearly enough:

Harmakhis flew in a ship and he landed by the city of Horus' throne. Thus spake Thoth: the sender of light, who is born of Ra, he has defeated the enemy. He is to be known from this day on as the sender of light, who is born of the mountain of light. Thus spake Harmakhis to Thoth: Bring this sun disk to all the cities of the gods in Lower Egypt, and all the cities of the gods in Upper Egypt and all the cities of the gods.[6]

Here and There

The phrase *sender of light,* which I have used here, is not one of my own creations. It comes from the text of Professor Heinrich Brugsch, who translated the Edfu text in 1870(!). So what have the sensible and rational Egyptologists—all of them loyal and obedient to their school of thinking and the zeitgeist—made of the winged sun disk? Ceremonial oddments. The original meaning is gone. It was no fantasy or dream of the uneducated Egyptians; it was simply what we would today describe as a UFO! Incapable or recognizing the original reality, academic doctrine transforms the former truth into myth. And now the world is all right again. Really?

A friend of mine, who is an Egyptologist, once told me that the thought that some god had actually intervened in a human conflict, was simply unbearable. Just as unbearable as my belief that extra-terrestrials had at some time taken a hand in Earthly affairs. Human logic, however, is sometimes prepared to make quite unexpected leaps. In the Old Testament, for instance, God—descending in a swathe of smoke, fires, and cataclysmic roars—often takes a hand to assist his chosen people in their struggles. Yes, in actual fact! Here the logic is watertight. Really?

What does the winged sun disk in Egypt have to do with Central America?

In 1860, not far from the village of Santa Lucia Cotzumalguapa in Guatemala (on the Pacific coast), a number of magnificent stelae were found during clearance work. The news reached an Austrian research-er, Dr. Habel, who traveled to Mexico in 1862 to visit the excavation site. Dr. Habel made some sketches and showed them to the director of the Royal Museum of Ethnology in Berlin, Dr. Adolf Bastian. Four years later, he himself travelled to Guatemala and bought all the old stone fragments from the owner of the finca where the stelae were found. Transporting these incredibly heavy stelae to Europe was a logistic headache. In the end, they decided to cut the stone monsters in half and transported them to the harbor of San José, 50 miles away. To make the blocks lighter, they hollowed out the rear sides. During the loading, one of the stelae broke free and sank into the harbor waters—where it still lies today. The remaining art-works from this forgotten age can be admired in the Ethnology Museum in the west of Berlin. Because archaeologists always have to label and categorize everything (otherwise they can't exhibit the artifacts), the stelae

3.5. The so-called "Ode to the Sun God." Author's own image.

were given a rather apt name: Ode to the Sun God. And indeed, you can clearly see a flying creature, swathed in flames, descending to the frightened folk below. You really can't miss the sun disk!

Extraterrestrial Technology

In the Edfu text about the winged sun disk, the term *sender of light* crops up. Or course, that's nothing any rational Egyptologist can work with. What actually is a "sender of light"? Has the term been wrongly interpreted? There are, in all probability, dozens if not hundreds of depictions of these "senders of light," but we do not recognize them because—as the biblical prophet Ezekiel said—we have eyes to see but do not see.

In the Temple of Seti I (also known as Sethos) in Abydos, the goddess Isis handed the pharaoh a strange object. This object must have been something really exceptional; otherwise it would hardly have been attributed directly to the goddess. What's more, this object is, in terms of dimensions, bigger than the pharaoh himself. Egyptologists call this object a Djed pillar. These Djed pillars have been found in various sizes throughout the whole of Egypt, and no one, thus far, has been able to come up with a plausible explanation. Depictions of the Djed pillar were even found under the very oldest of the pyramids, that of Djoser in Saqqara. The pillar must have been something quite special because even in the earliest ages of the old empire there was a priesthood of the "venerable Djed." In Memphis there was even a special ritual for the "erection of the Djed,"[7] which was carried out by the pharaoh with the assistance of his priests. Much later, after the original gods had disappeared and the pharaohs had been named the "sons of gods," no one remembered what the Djed pillars actually were. The important thing was that it had something to do with the gods. That was all that mattered. Consequently, depictions of the Djed pillar can be found in countless variations: on temple walls, in crypts, on treasure chests, and even on vases. Djed pillars are just as common in Egypt as winged suns. The only problem is that not a single expert has come up with a plausible explanation for the original meaning of this mysterious object. I have read in the literature that the Djed pillar was: a symbol of permanence, a symbol for eternity, a prehistoric fetish, a defoliated tree, a notched post, a fertility symbol, a spike, and so on.

What about something else? What about a "sender of light"? At least that's what it looks like. Crazy? When I look at all those hokey interpretations of this curious object, I could almost laugh. What actually has to happen before we open our eyes and see things for what they really are? Looking at the Djed pillar as a representation of a technological device seems more plausible to me than claiming it is some kind of "prehistoric fetish" or a "fertility symbol"! After all, the Djed pillar was not the only object that the gods gave to mankind. Another one is the Ark of the Covenant mentioned in the Old Testament. You can read all about it in the Bible. Moses received extremely precise instructions on how to construct a technical object from his "god" (Leviticus, chapter 25 ff.). There was an original of this object; Moses was merely expected to make a copy: "And see that thou make them after their pattern, which hath been showed thee in the mount" (Exodus 25:40).

3.6. Transporting the Ark of the Covenant (an illustration from an old bible). Author's own image.

Afterward, Aaron, Moses' brother, was told to form a priesthood to look after this device. So there was a team of specialists—just like the priesthood of the Djed pillar. A "sender of light" belonging to the gods was not something that could be entrusted to just anyone. It was dangerous. Just like the Ark of the Covenant.

Shortly after the construction of the Ark was completed, God warned his servant Moses that he must ensure that Aaron follow explicit instructions "or he will die" (Leviticus 16:2). Later the Ark of the Covenant was involved in a number of catastrophes. The Philistines captured the Ark (first book of Samuel, Chapter 4 ff.) and all the gawkers who got anywhere near the uncanny object died of diseases that today would probably be described as radiation sickness. The nails on their hands and feet fell off, as did their hair, their skin was covered in "boils," and "the men who did not die were smitten with tumors and the cry of the city went up to heaven" (I Samuel 5:12).[8] The bible even tells us about a fatal accident suffered by a priest who forgot to follow the strict safety guidelines: "...when they came to the threshing floor of Nacon, Uzzah reached out toward the ark of God and took hold of it.... And the anger of the Lord was kindled against Uzzah; and God smote him there for his error; and he died there by the ark of God" (II Samuel 6:6 ff.).

Poor old Uzzah! And he was one of the priests! So what did he do that was so wrong? And what kind of god smites one of his subjects for a moment of carelessness? The Bible provides an answer: "And the whole of mount Sinai was clad in smoke, because the Lord descended upon it in fire; and the smoke climbed up like the smoke from a furnace, and the whole mount quaked greatly" (Exodus 19:18).

This same God demanded sacrifices from the Israelites (gold, silver, precious stones) and iterated to his servant Moses that he should make it tell the Israelites in no uncertain terms: "You have seen that I have talked with you from heaven" (Exodus 20:22).

(You can find out more about what happened to the Ark of the Covenant and where the remains of this technical device can be found today in one of my earlier books, *Signs of the Gods.*[9])

Parts of the Old Testament (Bible), the Vedas (India), the pyramid texts (Egypt), the Apocrypha (such as the Book of Enoch), and Popol Vuh make more sense when viewed from a contemporary standpoint, and they complement each other in many areas. But when it comes to the Mayan Popol Vuh it becomes incredibly complicated. There are good reasons for this. The book was translated (into German, my native language) by a certain Dr. Wolfgang Cordan, who was fluent in a number of Mayan dialects. He called the text the *Book of the Council.*[10] That was 50 years ago. Cordan's translation was in a flowing style of speech, easily readable by anyone who chose to. The following generation of Maya experts did not accept Cordan's work and drew up a new translation, this time word for word.[11] To understand this version, you need to have lived with the K'iche' Maya for some time because there is simply endless room for interpretation. What did they really mean? How can we understand this text? Well, for a start, we have to bear in mind that there is no such thing as an "original" text of Popol Vuh. All of the translations are based on a single version that admittedly existed in the K'iche' language but wasn't actually written down until the 18th century by a Christian cleric, Father Francisco Ximénez. To represent the K'iche' sounds in a way that his contemporaries could read them, the priest used the Latin alphabet. He had to render K'iche' words, which may be pronounced in a drawn-out, sing-song manner, phonetically using Latin letters. Easier said than done. Here are a few extracts from the literal translation:[12]

"Sovereign and Quetzal Serpent, they who have borne children... luminous they are in the water...."

"The face of the Earth was not far for him. Nor was Xibalba (hell, the underworld) far for him. In an instant, he could return to the sky with Huracan...."

"Then they arose as the central lights. They arose straight into the sky.... Thus was the womb of the sky illuminated over the face of the Earth, for they came to dwell in the sky.... The four hundred boys who had died at the hands of Zipacna also rose up to become their companions. They became a constellation of the sky."

"...the miraculous power and the spirit essence...Sovereign and Quetzal Serpent. Thus their countenances appeared like people. People they came to be. They were able to speak and converse. They were able to look and listen...straightaway their vision came to them...."

And so on!

It's pretty hard to translate this mush into comprehensible English. If I were to try, I would end up with a version that had little to do with the original. But I can say this much: just like in the Bible, Popol Vuh tells of a confusion of languages. The people could no longer understand each other because of a "stone that changed their speech when they came from Tulan." We read about "valuable metals" that are to be given to certain gods (but also men). There are descriptions of "black people and white people," of boys that were sacrificed, of a mountain called "Hacavitz" where the people multiplied, and so on, and so on. It's a thoroughly mixed bag that arose from the impotence of language.

The vocabulary of the early chroniclers was limited. Many of the terms they used derived from their daily lives and regular natural events: Tribe and family, animals and plants, early devices and simple weapons all had names. There were words for sun, water, day and night, sunrise and sunset, lightning, thunder, birth, illness, and death. But any time something happened that could not be directly described with this sparse collection of words, then it was time to paraphrase and describe so that the available words could be made to evoke the event in the mind's eye.

However, language—words arranged one after another—cannot always express the meaning that is intended. Gestures are just as much a part of our communication process as pictures are or music is. At an auction, when someone raises a hand with five fingers, he is signaling to his partner in the first row that he wants to raise his bid by 50,000 dollars. Not a sound needs to be uttered. We cannot know which gestures the old story-tellers of the K'iche' Maya used to tell their tales. A laugh, a whine, a grimace, and a stamped foot may all have been used to change the sense of the actual series of words used. I remember once meeting a senn (a mountain herder) in an Alpine hut. He told me a tale of dwarves that, so he claimed, still lived right there in the region. When the words failed him, he gesticulated meaningfully. I could understand him. Without words.

This nonlinguistic component of communication—gestures, intonation, music, sadness, anger, happiness, or facial expressions—cannot be expressed by the simple spoken word. Spoken language is the poor relation of thought. It lumbers along after the event and has to invent new terms—words—for things that have already happened. Language is not a dogma of eternal values; it is a constantly evolving organism. Depending on the state of development of the user, language is never completely free of values; it is constantly adapting to the zeitgeist. Now, myths belong to the barely researched epochs of our past history. So, bearing that in mind, how many times may these first-used words have changed their meaning since then? Not only that, all those who recorded the myths in the first place filled their words with other semantic meaning. Back in the early days of language—let's not forget!—there simply were no words for the impossible. Of course, a Stone Age man would have no words to describe a helicopter, headlamps, pistols, an aircraft or a space shuttle, a protective space suit, or an ear-splitting UFO, but he knew words like *fire, lightning, earth-shaking, noise,* and *heat.* And then he was forced to use these to describe the impossible event he was experiencing. This is how, in Central America, the myth of the feathered serpent arose—something that was well-known in Egypt, too, by the way. For instance, in the grave of Seti I in the Valley of the Kings you can see many depictions of snakes with wings.

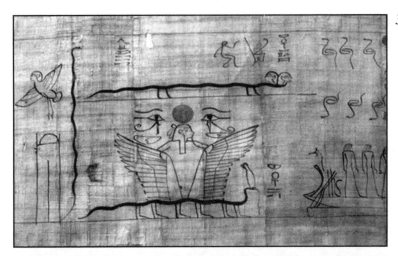

3.7.

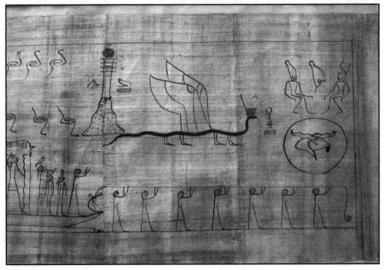

3.8.

Winged snakes in ancient Egyptian tombs. Images courtesy of Tatjana Ingold, Solothurn, Switzerland.

3.9. Another ancient Egyptian winged snake. Author's own image.

Thousands of years later, in our Age of Reason, the serious and rational world of science does not want to accept that Stone Age man could realistically have had any meetings with a high-tech civilization, and that he could have seen any helicopter-like flying machine or met with beings that they, in their ignorance, named gods. When even the original texts are utterly confusing—because of the incomprehensible terms and missing gestures—then the translations are bound to end up as some kind of religious-psychological mishmash. The methodologies simply do not allow any other possibilities. Total chaos!

E tana Over the Earth

Then there is the well-known myth of Etana, once part of the clay-tablet library of the Assyrian king Ashurbanipal (685–circa 627 BC). Found during excavations in Niniveh, the tablets are now kept in the British Museum in London. The origin of the story is unknown, although parts of it are present in the older Gilgamesh epic. The story tells how Etana is carried high up into the sky by an eagle. The magnificent bird repeatedly asks him to look down:

...After flying on high for some time, the eagle addresses Etana:

Look, my friend, how the Earth appears, look at the sea at the side of the world mountain.

And the Earth appeared as a mountain, the sea as a pool....

After flying on even higher, the eagle addresses Etana:

Look, my friend, how the Earth appears. And the Earth appeared as a plantation of trees....

My friend, look down and see how the Earth appears. And the Earth appeared as a garden, and the wide sea no bigger than a bucket.

And he carried him yet higher still and said: My friend, look down and see how the Earth disappears.

I looked down and saw how the Earth had disappeared and my eyes could not even pick out the wide sea.

My friend, I cannot go any further towards heaven. Stop now that I might return to the Earth....[13]

"The Eagle has landed" was the message sent back to Houston by the crew of *Apollo 11*, as they became the first men to set foot on the Moon. The eagle has landed. Even if the word *heaven* is used in the Etana epos, it is clear that what is being referred to here is space travel. After all, the eagle carries his burden up into the stratosphere (*"the wide sea [was] no bigger than a bucket"*) and up over the Earth (*"I looked down and saw how the Earth had disappeared...."*). And now we bundle it all up in our convoluted religious-psychological contemporary thinking because things that don't fit in simply cannot be.

So, you can see that we're not going to get any further by simply applying the old methods and old thinking. It seems to me that the real opponents of insight can be found within the ranks of science.

Stone Age man created his godly images all over the world. The faithful followers of the established religions call these images idols if they don't fit in with their own religious preconceptions. These pictures— grotesque faces, unimaginable beings with tongues of fire, beasts, and monsters—have been created by every culture from the depths of their own imaginations. Different and yet all the same—much like the language—but where is the origin of these artistically portrayed gods?

Many centuries ago, Amr ibn Luhai, a traveler throughout Arabia, told of men who produced or worshipped graven images. He asked them what was the source of this worship. This was the answer he received: "The pictures are the lords which we have prepared in accordance with their heavenly forms and persons."[14]

The "father of history-writing," the Greek Herodotus (ca. 490–425 BC) himself, said much the same. In the second book of his *Histories,* he told about his visit to Thebes (chapters 141 and 142) and how the priests explained 341 statues to him:

They demonstrated then that all the people portrayed by these statues were mortal beings, bearing no relation to gods. They claimed, however, that before these men, gods had been kings of Egypt—that they had lived alongside human beings.... The Egyptians claim to have precise knowledge of all this, because they have always kept count of and continuously chronicled the passing years....[15]

Originally, the Earth was home to cavemen, then gods and then crossbreeds (in other words, the sons and daughters of gods), then came mankind, as we know it today, and finally the gods disappeared—but not before promising to return one day in the far future. Men fashioned pictures, statues, or—depending on the level of their development—cave paintings of these gods, but they all had the same thought in the back of their minds: the Maya, the Egyptians, the Indians, and all the others. What they depicted were the inexplicable, grandiose-seeming, and transfigured beings from another world. But they were once real: They really were active among the Stone Age peoples.

The same applies to the temples! Originally, these "heavenly forms" served as the inspiration for the temples. Mankind has always imitated that which it admired, but also that which it didn't understand. These shrines were attractively built because the primitives hoped that the real gods would approve and come down and protect the human community from its enemies. That, of course, was often the spark that prompted the building of settlements in the surrounding areas. The priesthood did its work to ensure that faith in the gods—as well as fear of divine retribution—did not wane. The rest is history.

This claim is easy enough to prove and anyone can understand it, as long as the links to other cultures are made. Without these links, without the comparative mythology we will probably continue to flounder around in the dark. In the 25 nonfiction books I've written so far, I have provided hundreds of attestable items of evidence. Here are some examples:

- Wall paintings in the Sahara (Tassili), Brazil (Ceta Cidades at Piripiri), the United States (Hopi lands), Australia (Arnhem Land at Nourlangie and the Kimberley Ranges), Canada (Vancouver Island), and many more show a particularly international consistency when it comes to representing the gods.

- Dogu figures from Japan look very much the same as statues of gods from Colombia, Peru, and Bolivia.

- The straw suits worn by the Brazilian Kayapo tribesmen reflect their tribal memory of the their heavenly teachers, as do the kachina dolls of the Hopi people in Arizona.

All this and much more, and none of this has any weight? We can't view this as proof?

"If you examine the theories propounded by Erich von Däniken with an open and impartial mind, then you'll see that nothing in these hypotheses really contradicts the strictest rules of science or our understanding of the universe."

—Professor Luis Navia,
Professor of Philosophy
at the New York Institute of Technology

Those extraterrestrials—the misunderstood gods of ancient times—promised that they would return to Earth. This promised return was immortalized in the Maya mythology and in the Maya calendar. But the Mayans weren't the only ones waiting for a second coming. There is a "Judgment Day" coming.

IMAGES FROM PUMA PUNKU

A statue of Pachamama, the Andean fertility goddess

These steps at the ruins of Puma Punku once stood under water. They were coated in a fine layer of lime scale.

The central god on the Gateway of the Sun at Puma Punku.

The walls around the temple Kalasasaya (above) have been reconstructed. The heads that were mounted on the wall during reconstruction had originally been somewhere else.

Image courtesy of Tatjana Ingold

Visitors to Puma Punku have marveled at the size and detail of the ruins. "Each slab is a masterpiece," says author Erich von Daniken (below far right).

DO ANCIENT CARVINGS, DRAWINGS, AND FIGURES SHOW MAN'S ENCOUNTERS NOT WITH GODS, BUT WITH OTHER BEINGS FROM ABOVE?

Right: Hybrids on the Black Obelisk of Shalmaneser Below: Isis hands Seti the Djed pillar in the temple in Abydos.

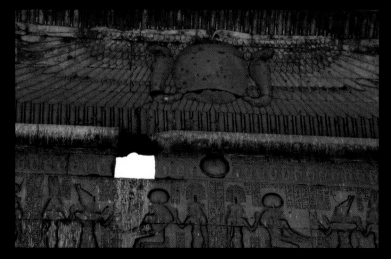

Above right: Dogu figure from Japan
Right: Winged sun disk at Dendera, Egypt

Chapter 4

The Return of the Gods

4.1. The inscription on Monument No. 6 in Tortuguero. Author's own image.

This picture shows a Mayan inscription on Monument No. 6 in Tortuguero. It's a small place in the Mexican state of Tabasco, around 50 miles northwest of Palenque. Any Maya specialist can read the inscription. You start at the top left with the first glyph, then move right to the second, then down to the second line from left to right. The Maya experts read:

"tzuhtzajoom / u yuxlajuun bak'tun chan ajaw / ux uniiw…"

"It will be ended / the 13th bak'tun 4 ajaw / 3 uniww / it will happen (next glyph is broken off) / Bolon Yokte will descend to..." (next glyph missing).

So some god called "Bolon Yokte" will come down to Earth on a certain day. If we convert this date to our calendar, it's December 23, 2012. What can we expect then on this date? And who is this "Bolon Yokte"?

The very same Bolon Yokte appears on the so-called "Vase of the Seven Gods." Here he is praised repeatedly as a "holy one," a "divine being" who was involved in the creation of the world. Bolon Yokte was even involved at the very beginning of the Mayan calendar, on August 13, 3114 BC. And in Temple No. XIV in Palenque, Bolon Yokte also appears in connection with an event that unfortunately cannot be deciphered from the glyphs. Either way, this unknown event happened on the incredible date of July 29, 931,449 BC—the date is clearly readable. In other words, it happened long before there were any Mayans around. Bolon Yokte also appears on page 60 of the Dresden Codex, one of the very few handwritten Mayan documents to survive the Spanish destruction, and yet again in the "Chilam Balam books." These were manuscripts written by priests, but not until after the Spanish conquest.

Bolon Yokte is always mentioned in connection with great power. He must have been one of these mighty, awe-inspiring unknown beings that men could not otherwise explain. Bolon Yokte is not the only one who features in tales of second comings of the so-called gods; one can also infer the return of the gods from the Mayan calendar. How does that work then?

Several of the glyphs on the Tortuguero monument feature squiggles and vertical strokes. These are Mayan numbers. They are as ever-present in the Mayan world as the winged sun disk in Egypt. To at least understand the main track—that is, the one concerned with the return of the gods—you ought to know a little bit about the downfall of the Mayan culture and also how the Mayan calendar works. (I dealt exhaustively with this subject in one of my earlier books, *Der Tag, an dem die Götter kamen.*)

Brutal Conquerors

On Saturday, November 15, 1519, Spanish conquistador Her-nando Cortés (1485–1547) waited with his forces a short distance away from Tenochtitlan. Set in the middle of a glittering silver lagoon, the city towered proudly with its mysterious and arcane temples, palaces, columns, and sparkling pyramid towers. Clothed in the magnificent uniform of an admiral, Cortés strode to the front of his small company. Crossbowmen and horses rode at the flanks—colorful streamers and flags fluttering from their lances—an honor guard for the future conqueror as he drew into the broad avenida in Tenochtitlan.

The Aztec leader, Moctezuma, came down to greet the stranger, carried on a jewel-laden, gold-plated sedan by slaves who had lain out a long cotton carpet along the route. Cortés swung down from his steed, never taking his eyes off the Aztec leader for a second. C.W. Ceram wrote about this meeting in his world famous book on archeology, *Gods, Graves and Scholars*:

> For the first time during the great history of discovery, it so happened that someone from the Christian occident no longer needed to reconstruct a rich, foreign culture from the rubble of its remains, but rather was able to encounter it in the flesh. Cortés stood before Moctezuma—it was as if Brugsch-Bey suddenly bumped into Ramses, or Koldewey met Nebuchadnezzar during a stroll through the hanging gardens of Babylon, and they had been able, like Cortés and Moctezuma, to speak freely with each other.[1]

Moctezuma was, at that time, lord over 200,000 warriors. Despite the Spanish cannons, they could have destroyed the interlopers with ease. Why didn't Moctezuma choose to fight? Why did he rather choose the route of subservience?

The answer lies perhaps in the Aztec religion—the same one, by the way, practiced by the Maya. The difference between the Aztecs and Maya is predominantly a geographical one: The Aztecs lived in the highlands; the Maya in the lowlands. And just as the Jews await the return of the Messiah, the Moslems for their Mahdi, and the Inca their god Viracocha, the son of the sun, like the South Sea islanders yearned for the return of their god of reward, or the Egyptians for the return of Osiris (from the constellation of Orion), so too waited the Aztecs and Maya for the return of their bringer of salvation, the "Quetzal Serpent."

The Aztecs and the Maya lived according to precise calendar cycles. Buildings were erected in harmony with the calendrical rhythm, and feast days organized according to the calendar. (We do just the same today. Christian festivals like Easter, Whitsun, and Christmas are dominant aspects of our year, and for our international sport events, such as the Olympic Games or the FIFA World Cup, huge infrastructures of new buildings are constructed.) As luck would have it, Cortés's arrival coincided with the end of a calendar period—a time when expectations were traditionally high that the quetzal serpent would finally return. The priests had preached of the event for a long time. And now, finally, the event that the legends had all foretold now also matched the date. The devout high priest Moctezuma could have, may have, or even must have recognized Cortés, this bearded white man, as at least an emissary of the "Quetzal Serpent."

So he received his foreign guest with pomp and ceremony, and even offered him his palace to live in. Cortés enjoyed this generous hospitality for three days, and then he demanded that a chapel be built. Willingly, Moctezuma assembled a team of Aztec artisans to build the Christian house of worship.

The Spaniards saw themselves as an occupying army—as indeed they were—and looked on suspiciously as the worked progressed. On one wall they discovered a freshly plastered spot and suspected that a secret door had been hidden behind it. Secretly, they broke through the wall and found themselves standing in a room filled with gold figures, bars of gold and silver, jewel-encrusted adornments, and fine materials woven with feathers. Cortés estimated the value of the find to be around 162,000 gold pesos (around 10 million dollars in today's money).

During a feast to honor the god Teocalli, the Spaniards waited tensely for a prearranged signal. When it finally came, they struck with deadly effect, murdering 700 unarmed Aztec nobles and priests without warning. The Aztecs lost patience with their leader and overthrew Moctezuma. After making his brother king, they stormed the palace where the Spaniards were quartered. Suddenly Tenochtitlan was thrown into bloody chaos. Cortés had his men burn down the temples and houses. While the Spaniards were abroad butchering the Aztecs with their superior weapons, none other than the toppled monarch Moctezuma, of all people, offered his services as an intermediary—the very idea! It was his last: On June 30, 1520, his outraged countrymen stoned him to death.

Cortés finally gave the order to pack up and carry off the treasure. Heavily laden with gold, silver, and precious jewels, the Spaniards planned to sneak out of Tenochtitlan. A watchman discovered the plunderers and gave out an alarm signal. The Aztecs set off hot on the heels of the Spaniards.

The Night of Sorrows

This was the *noche triste,* the night of sorrows, for the Spaniards. They fled in panic. The heavy gold and silver weighed them down heavily. They stumbled and fell; some even drowned in the swamp. Aztec warriors killed great numbers of them. Horses and riders rode through a storm of buzzing arrows; they were bombarded with stones from slingshots. Lances tipped with obsidian—a crystalline stone with a tendency to splinter—pierced the bodies of the hated occupiers. In that terrible night, Cortés' company was reduced by half; he himself was sorely wounded, and the large part of the treasure that had roused their avarice had sunk in the waters and quagmires of the lagoon. *Noche triste!*

Weeks later Cortés returned with well-armed reinforcements. King Cuauhtémoc, Moctezuma's nephew, was then ruler of Tenochtitlan. He made a good job of defending his city, but under a steady bombardment from the Spanish cannons and siege engines he was finally forced to capitulate. Cortés had free rein to tear apart the city to find its hidden treasures. Even under torture, though, Cuauhtémoc refused to reveal the location of the cache. So he was hanged. After all, this was not just gold, silver, and jewels, but also holy relics, manuscripts, and possibly even gifts from the gods. The Aztec treasure remained missing—to this very day.

Proud Tenochtitlan was finally conquered by the Spaniards in 1521. Its temples and pyramid, idols, stelae, and libraries were all buried in rubble and ash. Nowadays, Mexico City stands on the same site.

Decades followed, during which all of Central America remained under the yoke of Spanish rule. In a series of bloody battles across the lowlands, the Spaniards defeated one Maya tribe after the other. The intractable indigenous peoples were brutally tortured or often simply wiped out. They were forced to live under a reign of violence and terror, and soon—to add insult to injury—they also found themselves being struck down by epidemics. Before too long the Spaniards hardly had to lift a finger to conquer regions, or raze cities to the ground. As the old gods were forced to make way for the new religion under the sign of the cross, the Aztecs and Maya scattered in all directions of the compass. The once-grandiose palaces slowly crumbled. The greedy jungle of the hot and humid rainforest gradually swallowed up the pyramids, penetrated the temples, and pulled down the platforms. Snakes, jaguars, and other kinds of tropical fauna made the sites their homes. Documents of inestimable value merely rotted away, becoming food for the ants and beetles. And the sun finally set on a unique culture with untold knowledge about those gods of the past.

The Sign of the Cross

Ever more Spanish ships arrived in Central America: Hordes of adventurers, officials, treasure hunters and priests made the trip over the ocean. It was all about gold and christianization. Thirty years after the destruction of Tenochtitlan, a certain young Spaniard arrived in the New World. His name was Fray Diego de Landa. He was born in 1524 to noble parents in Cifuentes in the province of Guadalajara in Spain. This was the time of the church's great expansion, and it was accepted practice for all rich families to send one son or daughter into the church. Diego de Landa started his life in the Franciscan monastery in San Juan de los Reyes at the tender age of 16. Totally devoted to Christ, he prepared for his mission with a program of asceticism. Diego was just 25 years old when he was assigned to a group of young monks whose task it was to convert 300,000 natives on the Yucatán peninsula. Intelligent and infused with the urge to serve Christ to the best of his ability, the young Diego learned the Mayan language in just a few months so that he was already able to deliver his sermons and holy dogma in Mayan by the time he arrived in the Yucatán.

No wonder, then, that Diego was seen as a high flier. In no time at all he was made manciple of the new monastery in Izamal and started setting up satellite missions. After all, the land cost them nothing— they had taken it from the Indios—and slave labor was easy enough to come by. Diego de Landa dressed in rough, woolen robes and personally monitored the education of the young Indios. Those converted to Christianity were soon filled with the same zeal as their master and destroyed the old shrines with the same enthusiasm that filled him.

Diego looked with great interest at the mighty buildings of T'ho, seeing them, however, only as sources of stone for the construction of the new Christian city of Mérida. Thus the Maya temples became Christian cathedrals; the pyramids became the administration buildings for the Spanish rulers. Despite the fact that millions of polished stones were dragged to the new construction sites, Diego de Landa doubted that the "supply of buliding material could ever be exhausted."[2]

The holy zealot Diego de Landa was finally made provincial head of the order of Franciscans, before finally being made bishop of the new Christian city of Mérida. It made him furious when he saw Mayans still clinging to their old culture and rites—when they were not prepared to let go of their old gods. Thus he gave the order to destroy all Mayan idols and writings. July 12, 1562, was certainly a day to remember: 5,000 icons, 13 altars, 192 ritual vessels, and 27 scientific and religious works, along with other illustrated manuscripts, were piled up in front of the church of San Miguel in Mani. At Diego de Landa's order, the whole pile was set alight. The flames licked, devoured, and consumed all of those irreplaceable documents of a grandiose culture. Ironically, the name of the city, Mani, translates as "it's over."

Unbothered by his act of cultural destruction, Diego de Landa noted: "We found a large number of books with illustrations, but these contained only lies and devilry. We burned them all, which sorely aggrieved the Maya causing them to sorrow greatly."[3]

That sorrow lasts to this day—and not only among Maya researchers, but also authors like me. If only we still had access to those old texts.... Then we wouldn't need to arduously scrabble around search for clues so that we can painstakingly revive the knowledge that existed thousands of years ago in Egypt and India, and hundreds of years ago in Central America, and that was part of the established wisdom of the scholars of those times—for instance, knowledge about the visits by genuine gods (= extraterrestrials) during the Stone Age.

The auto-da-fé in Mani was just the start signal. In their blind zeal, the missionaries burned Maya manuscripts wherever they found them. Using the justification that it was "the Devil's work," Bishop de Landa destroyed every trace of Mayan culture that was connected to the gods, just like in Peru and Bolivia (see Chapter 1).

Mayan Writings

Despite this—and it's certainly a little joke of history—who do Maya researchers have to thank for delivering the keys to Mayan mathematics and the Mayan calendar? None other than the merciless Diego de Landa. For without him we would not know the Mayan calendar or its numerical system, and we would know nothing about the return of the gods. "How did that happen?" you ask.

Well, Bishop Diego de Landa—today he would be described as the hawk among the missionaries—somehow got caught in the firing line of the Spanish court. Informers brought back news to faraway Spain that Diego had even burned objects made of gold. Finding himself suddenly under pressure, Diego de Landa sought allies in the New World, allies who introduced him to the secrets of Maya knowledge. His teachers were the sons of the indigenous noble families. They were converts to Christianity and taught Bishop de Landa everything they had learned from their parents—one piece at a time. Diego de Landa noted everything down in Latin. He learned about the Mayan numeric system and the calendar, and also how their alphabet worked. And thus came about a veritable apologia with the title *Relación de las cosas de Yucatán*—a report on things in the Yucatán.[4] This text turned out to be a highly important source for Maya research. And it was rediscovered by pure chance.

Three hundred years (!) later, Abbé Charles-Etienne Brasseur (1814–1874), a cleric working in the Royal Library in Madrid, discovered a rather unimposing document tucked between two gold-embossed folios. Brasseur, who himself had been a missionary for many years in Guatemala, was fascinated. Mayan glyphs and sketches stood out from the small, black Latin letters. In addition to these were a number of squiggles and short dashes, as well as short strokes placed over each other. By sheer coincidence, Brasseur had found the key that opened up the way out of the jungle of Maya numbers and letters.

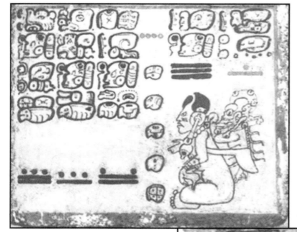

4.2.

*Folios from the
Madrid Codex.
Author's own
images.*

4.3.

Bishop Diego de Landa had written in his apologia: "The most important thing the tribal chiefs carried around with their territories were their scientific books."[5]

His countryman, José de Acosta, went further: "In the Yucatán there were bound and folded books in which the Indios stored their knowledge of the planets, nature and their ancient lore."[6]

Only four Maya manuscripts from pre-Spanish times survived the destruction in Central America. They are known as codices, and they can be found today in Mexico City, Madrid, Paris, and Dresden. The Madrid Codex was found by Abbé Brasseur, the same man who found the text by Diego de Landa, in the possession of a professor from Madrid's school for diplomats. The Paris Codex was discovered in a waste paper basket of the Parisian National Library, and the Dresden Codex was brought to Dresden from Italy by Johann Christian Götze, a librarian from the Royal Library. That was back in 1739. Götze wrote at the time:

> Our Royal Library now has the advantage over many others, for it possesses a rare treasure. It was discovered in private hands in Vienna, and had been kept more by chance as its owner did not suspect its worth. Without doubt, it is from the estate of some Spaniard who was either in America himself or one of his ancestors was.[7]

Did not suspect its worth? Phew! These days the Dresden Codex is worth several million dollars.

The fourth of the Maya manuscripts is called the Grolier Codex. It consists of 11 incomplete pages that discuss the planet Venus.

All of the Maya texts are written on thin parchments made of bast fiber from the wild fig trees that grew in the area. Originally, the bark of the trees would have been made more elastic by treating it with the sap of the rubber tree. Then it would have been painted with starch from vegetable tubers and laid out to dry before being painted in four colors using soft feathers. Finally the manuscripts were folded in a concertina-like fashion.

The age of the Mayan manuscripts is unknown. If they are copies of older documents (as is likely) their content could be at least 2,000 years old (if not more!). The Paris Codex contains prophecies, the Madrid Codex is a horoscope, apparently, and the Dresden Codex is filled with mathematical and astronomical relationships. All are now readable, thanks to Bishop Diego de Landa, who provided us with the key to the Mayan numerical system.

The Dresden Codex

Maya scholars have been trying to crack the codices for two hundred years. The meticulous academics have been able to reconstruct much—but just as much remains shrouded in the mists of interpretation. Professor Thomas Barthel, an expert in Maya writing systems, talks of an "evident mixed character"[8] because the same signs can sometimes mean completely different things. There are also blocks of hieroglyphics that are placed in the middle of a number text, or plays on words that "offer numerous different possibilities for interpretation whose senses are often completely at odds with one another."[9]

Nevertheless, what the academics *have* found is simply breathtaking. The Dresden Codex talks about Venus orbits, certain gods who are described as the "lords of the heavens," a thunder and lightning god, and of course the complicated Maya calendar. Maya academics have labeled the confusing panoply of gods with different letters. In the Dresden Codex, much is carried out by the gods A, D, E, and N, although it is often unclear which god is responsible for which deed. Six leaves of the Dresden Codex contain astronomical profiles of Venus, two leaves discuss the Martian orbit, and four the Jovian orbit and even its moons. Some of the pages are primarily concerned with the Moon, Mercury, and Saturn, but the constellations Orion, Gemini, and the Pleiades are also mentioned. Filled with complex calculations, the tables even present the reference points of the planets in relation to each other and their respective positions with regard to the Earth.

Then come periods of Mercury, Venus, Earth, and Mars years adding up to 135,200 days.[10] The ancient Maya even dealt with astronomical numbers of 400 million years.

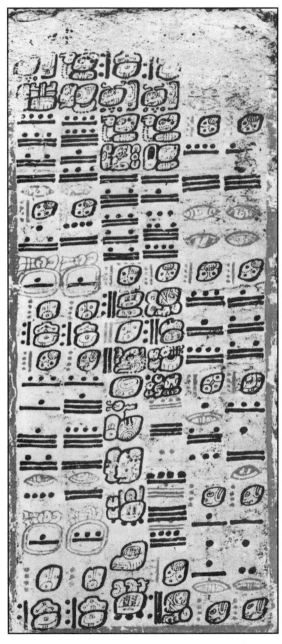

4.4. A page from the Dresden Codex filled with mathematical calculations. Author's own image.

The Maya astronomy documented in the Dresden Codex is not fully understood, even today. Several folios talk of battles between the planets,[11] and there are seven sheets of so-called eclipse tables containing the dates of every single eclipse from the past and the future. In 1938, Professor Herbert Noll Hussum, the best-known Dresden Codex specialist of the age, wrote: "The eclipse tables are so ingeniously drawn up that they contain not only every single possible eclipse visible in the area for hundreds of years, but also even the not directly observable, purely theoretical eclipses are given exactly—to the precise day."[12]

That observation was made 70 years ago. It still makes some Maya researchers uneasy. How could a culture that still practiced human sacrifice be such masters of astronomy, exhibiting skills that should have been far beyond their ken. Where did they get this knowledge? Where did the inspiration come from that told them that the planets had a predictable relationship to each other? Centuries of observations, a manic compulsion to create the perfect calendar, or even an addiction to mathematics does not explain this puzzle. As the Earth itself has an elliptical orbit around the Sun and, of course, the other planets are not actually standing still, every observation is susceptible to a certain time lag. Venus, for example, only appears in the same constellation once every eight years; Jupiter every 12 years. What's more, the Maya lived in a geographical area in which it was impossible to observe the stars at all for half the year. In the Dresden Codex, however, there are astronomical points of reference that only appear every 6,000 years! The Maya weren't even around for 6,000 years! Mere calculations are not enough to deduce that the orbit of Venus has to be "put back" a day every 6,000 years. Added to all this, the evidence points to the fact that the Maya were in possession of their astronomical knowledge from the very start—almost as if their tables and books of data and orbital calculations had just fallen to them out of the sky. One Maya specialist explained to me that these kinds of observations could be made in just a few decades. The Maya were a Stone Age people—have we forgotten that? They possessed no modern measurement devices, telescopes, or computers. Even the archaeological objection that the Mayan priest-astronomers on their tall pyramids would have been able to observe the starry skies without having to look through haze and clouds doesn't hold much water. The pyramid towers—such as those in Tikal (Guatemala)—were astronomically aligned at the very planning stage. The astronomical knowledge is, therefore, older than the pyramids themselves.

Where Does the Knowledge Come From?

Sixty years ago, respected astronomer Robert Henseling shocked the scientific community with some of his conclusions about Maya astronomy:

1. It must be considered impossible that the Mayans had instruments and methods at their disposal for the precise measurement of angles and time.

2. There can be no doubt, however, that the Maya astronomers had knowledge of star constellations from thousands of years in the past, which included reliable information on their type and position on certain calendar dates.

3. This is incomprehensible, unless corresponding observations had been made prior to this period—in other words, thousands of years before the beginning of the Christian calendar—*by somebody somewhere and reliably handed down for posterity* [author's emphasis].

4. Such achievements, however, are dependent on certain factors. *For instance, that in that very prior age there had been a development period of extremely long duration.* [author's emphasis].[13]

Since then, the scant number of experts who have worked on the Dresden Codex are hedgy about making any meaningful comments. I believe that the core of the astronomical knowledge of the Maya must be much older than the academics are willing to concede. Even in classical Greece, an empire rich in top-notch mathematicians and brilliant philosophers, it was sacrilege to assert that the Earth moved around the Sun. Anaxagoras (circa 500–428 BC) was accused of heresy and forced to flee his home town when he claimed that the Sun was nothing more than a glowing rock. Ptolemy of Alexandria (circa 90–168 AD), who had the benefit of the wisdom of hundreds of years of Egyptian and Babylonian astronomy at his disposal, placed the Earth at the center of his planetary system. It wasn't until Nicolaus Copernicus (1476–1543) came on the scene that there was any serious doubt of the matter. He postulated that it was in fact the Sun that was at the center point of our planetary orbits. After him came Giordano Bruno (1548–1600), Tycho Brahe (1546–1601), Johannes Kepler (1571–1630), and Galileo Galilei (1564–1642), until at last the structure of our solar system, as indeed it came to be called, and the elliptical orbits of the planets were finally fully understood. Yet we are expected to believe that the Stone Age people of the Maya tribes discovered all this in just a few centuries— *without any reliable instruments?*

Native American Traditions

It is hard to grasp: In Central America there existed an ancient, but highly precise, canon of astronomical knowledge, closely connected to the gods who, for their part, (a) came from "the heavens," (b) clearly were an awe-inspiring bunch, and (c) quite often pushed mankind around. This knowledge came from a god they called "Quetzal Serpent," although such a creature no more existed than a fire-breathing, flying dragon in China. The Mayans were by no means stupid. They wouldn't confuse a quetzal bird with a thundering feathered serpent.

This contradiction is simply not compatible with their astronomical expertise. On top of this, we shouldn't view the Maya knowledge in isolation; after all, their cousins, the native North Americans, lived close by. And they all knew the extraterrestrial quetzal serpent, even if it sometimes appeared in a slightly different form. The Tootooch Indians from the Pacific Northwest Coast, United States, called the quetzal serpent the "thunderbird." One of their totem poles for this thunderbird serves as the symbol for the "city of heavenly beings."[14] The same designation is used by the Canadian First Nations people in British Columbia. Here too the quetzal serpent is known as the thunderbird. It all seems so much more logical. The Pawnee tribe in today's Nebraska are convinced that man was created from the stars, and heavenly teachers came down regularly to Earth "to tell the men and women more about the things they needed to know."[15] We researchers of today treat the Maya wisdom in an isolated fashion, as if there had never been any other tribes or descendants in other regions that had maintained their lore and traditions in just the same way.

The creation myth of the Cherokee (northwest Georgia) starts this way: "In the beginning, all living things lived and dwelled above in the sky...the occupants of the sky home were anxious to get down for the sky home was getting more crowded all the time...."[16]

The Miccosukee tribe (South Florida) claim: "A long time ago, a tribe came down from the heavens to the Mikasuki swamps in the north of Florida. They swam on to the land and built the city of Mikasuki. The name of the Miccosukee Indians derives from this town."[17]

In British Columbia (Pacific Coast of Canada) the Salishan people tell: "Once the Earth people wanted to make war on the Sky people...."[18]

Also at home in Canada are the Ojibway tribe (Ontario, Canada). According to their lore, they also belong to the society of the "sky people."[19] These "sky people" are "not angels but humans with lighter skin and scarlet red tunics with hoods."[20]

And, of course, the Hopi Indians (Arizona) also speak of the "heavenly teachers."[21] They even make representations of these teachers in the form of dolls to this day.

These are just a few examples from the North American continent. I can't shake off the feeling that the academic Maya specialists view their quetzal serpent as something unique, but, after reading through the millennia-old legends and histories of other cultures, it has become clear to me that the gods from back then (that is, the extraterrestrials) shared a lot of knowledge with our forefathers—most notably in the field of astronomy. And there are even eye-witness accounts from people who were there at the time and wrote of their experiences.[22]

The Maya Calendar Wheels

The Mayan calendar—now decipherable thanks to Diego de Landa's basic research—now brings us to the next piece of craziness from this jungle people. Its smallest unit was a "week" with 13 days. Just imagine a small cogwheel with 13 teeth, engraved with the Maya numbers from 1 to 13. Next comes a "month" of 20 days—in our mind's eye, a cogwheel with 20 teeth. Now bring the small cog and the larger cog together and mark the zero position—on the small cog the point for "one"; on the larger one the Maya word *imix*. After 13 turns, the two wheels return to this start position. In total, 260 teeth have run through this cycle, equivalent to a Maya year with 260 days.

But—everybody knows this—a year doesn't have 260 days. It has 365 days. A 260-day calendar would be no use to man nor beast on our Earth. You couldn't mark off spring or fall; there'd be no fixed date for sowing or harvesting. To this day, no one knows why the Maya used a 260-day year. Therefore it is known as the "god year" or "holy year." Among the Maya it was known as *Tzolk'in*. All of the Mayans' religious rituals took place according to the rhythm of the *Tzolk'in,* all of their holy dates can be read from the *Tzolk'in*. For everyday use or agricultural purposes, though, the *Tzolk'in calendar* was useless.

The Maya astronomers knew this. After all they knew the exact orbital data of the Earth—with inexplicable precision. They had measured the exact length of our year to exactly 365.242129 days. That number is more precise than our own calendar! Just for comparison:

The Julian calendar	= 365.250000 days
The Gregorian calendar	= 365.242500 days
The Mayan calendar	= 365.242129 days
Absolute astronomical calculation	= 365.242189 days

There are always decimal places behind the point. We compensate for the inaccuracy in our calendar by adding an extra day every four years—what we call leap years. That's when those poor souls who are born on February 29th can finally celebrate their birthdays again! The Maya did it differently: They added an extra 13 days every 52 years and, with a number of other diverse tricks, managed to create the most precise calendar in the ancient world.

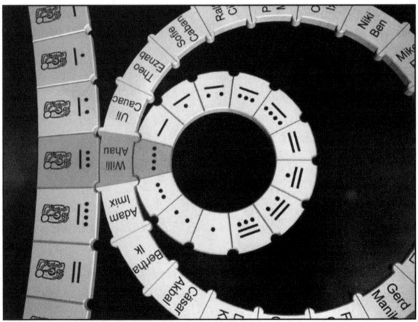

4.5. Three Maya calendar wheels. For clarity, names have been added next to the Maya words. Author's own image.

To the two cogwheels that represent the *Tzolk'in year* of 260 days, we must now add a third, larger cogwheel with 365 teeth. The Maya called their 365-day calendar *Haab*. Now we do the same thing as before, this time with three cogwheels. This time we draw a red mark on all three wheels at the zero position. How long will it take until all three cogwheels get back to their starting positions? (To simplify the process, I have added names next to the Maya words in image 4.5 shown on page 149.)

There are 18,980 teeth or days. Put another way, the 365-toothed wheel has turned 52 times; the 260-day wheel has turned 73 times. For the Maya, this meant 52 earthly years were equivalent to 73 god years. The Maya researchers even have a term for this period: a *calendar round*.

The Maya calculated with much greater calendar numbers than the 18,980 days of the calendar round. There are calendar calculations of 23,040,000,000 days or 64,109,589 years. Some inscriptions even extend 400 million years into the past. How was this possible with a calendar round of only 18,980 days? The solution is a fourth, even bigger cogwheel, which Maya researchers call the "long count." These four cogwheels begin in a start phase marked with the ominous glyphs "4 ahau 8 cumhu." The beginning of the Mayan calendar. But *when* in the dark mists of time did 4 ahau 8 cumhu take place? When did the Maya calendar start—in terms of our calendar, that is?

This is a question that has caused generations of historians many a sleepless night! On the basis of the religious festivals celebrated *after* the Spanish conquest, it was possible to count back. In the end, the experts agreed on a date: August 13, 3114 BC. This date was the definitive beginning of the Mayan calendar.

So far, so good. But *why* had the Mayans started their calendar on August 13, 3114 BC? Strictly speaking, according to accepted thinking, the Maya didn't even exist back then. In other words, the start date is older than the people themselves. Every culture has or had its own calendar, and the date on which it begins always marks some incredibly important event. For the Christians, it is the birth of Christ. That's where the counting starts. For the Muslims, it is the day on which Mohammed moved from Mecca to Medina (622 AD). The Jewish calendar begins with the creation of the world, 5770 years ago (3761 BC). So what happened to the forefathers of the Maya that was so unspeakably important that it caused them to start their calendar on August 13, 3114 BC?

The Maya have handed down the story in their legends, recorded for posterity in the Book of the Jaguar Priests. It is one of the so-called "Chilam Balam" books that were first written after the Spanish conquest. Luckily, the Spaniards didn't quite manage to wipe out every single one of the priests. A few managed to flee. Holed up in remote hiding places, they wrote down their ancient knowledge on the new paper. This was how the Chilam Balam books came about. You can read for yourself: "They descended from the street of the stars...they spoke the magic tongue of of the stars of heaven.... Yea, their sign is our certainty that they came from heaven.... And when they return, the thirteen gods and the nine gods, they will reorder what they once created."[23]

In Chapter 3, I talked about language, its meaning, and how it has developed and changed. In this quote from the Book of the Jaguar Priests it must be obvious to even the most ignorant layman that the word *heaven* used here is a synonym for the term *space*.

From an *earthly point of view*—in other words, in terms of sowing and harvesting—the monumental Maya cycles made no sense at all. They did in the minds of the Maya. After 37,960 days, for example, the gods started their journey to their great resting place. Applying statements such as these to the Quetzal Serpent (that is, spacecraft) may well make sense, but it makes no sense at all if the quetzal serpent is merely a reference to the quetzal bird.

The Return of Bolon Yokte

Having fixed the start date of the Maya calendar at August 13, 3114 BC, we can now start playing with our cogwheels again. How long will it take until all of the cogwheels of the long count get back to their starting positions? Working that out in today's computer age is a mere trifle. We know the start date and we know how many teeth are on the cogs. If we transfer the result to our calendar, we see that the Maya calendar comes to an end on Sunday, December 23, 2012. That is when the gods are expected to return from their long journey. This is what the inscription on Monument No. 6 in Tortuguero tells us (see the start of this chapter for more). It seems that Bolon Yokte is coming back.

One of the Maya people's main gods is known by the experts as "Lady Beastie." Her birth date is given as December 7, 3121 BC—in other words, *six years before* the start of the Maya calendar. Lady Beastie is not the only one of the Mayan gods to have come to Earth *before* the start of the Mayan calendar: There are a number of others, too. In Temple No. XIV in Palenque, Bolon Yokte appears with a deed that took place on the unimaginable date of July 29, 931,449 BC. How did this date come about if the Maya didn't start counting until August 13, 3114 BC?

Well, it's like this: The calendar may start on August 13, 3114 BC, but Maya used a special glyph to show what happened *before* or after the start of their calendar—just as we use the abbreviation BC to describe events that took place before the start of the Christian calendar. But the $64,000 question is this: What's going to happen on Sunday, December 23, 2012? Will Bolon Yokte and his cohort of Mayan gods really come back down to Earth? Will we experience a "god shock" in a couple of years? How can we prepare for this?

Prepare? I recommend this book! What else? And what about December 23, 2012? Will this day be a catastrophe for mankind? Well, before we can claim anything like that we'd need to be sure as hell that it's the right date and—despite the Mayan cogwheels—we're certainly not. Maya specialists spent years arguing *when* the Mayan calendar began. The theories covered everything from 8498 BC to 3114 BC. The only thing the experts could really agree on, was that whichever starting point they took it would be before the Mayans even existed. They finally settled for August 13, 3114 BC, because they were able to recalculate religious Maya dates noted during the age of the Spanish conquistadores. So is this date really final and definite? Well, I wouldn't swear to it.

Miscalculation?

How does this relate then to our calendar? Put it this way: I'm sitting here in the year 2009, typing this book into my computer. Two thousand and nine: That's the number of years that are supposed to have passed since Jesus was born in a lowly cattle shed in Bethlehem. Assuming that the early Christians didn't start counting until 20 years *after* Jesus' birth, our calendar would be 20 years short. Twenty years that exist nowhere. The number 2009 would be wrong. The conversion of the Maya calendar to the Christian calendar is not based on the effective time that has past, but on the actual *dates we use.* Two thousand and nine is just a number—a number that does not necessarily actually represent the number of years that have really past. And if the number 2009 isn't right—because a number of years were not even counted— then the number 2012 can't be right either. On top of that, we're not even totally sure which calender corrections were carried out in the early middle ages.

If we accept that the early Christians left out 20 years, then the correct date today—in terms of actual *elapsed time* and not simply the *year date*—would be 2029, not 2009. In that case, the start date of 3114 BC calculated for the Maya calendar would be wrong. Why? Because all the calculations are based on the year dates and not the effectively elapsed time. The calculations run either from before Christ's birth or after it. Regardless of which direction you go, you're still missing 20 years in your calculation. If 20 years after Christ were missing, and in truth 2029 years had actually passed, then the ominous year 2012—the year in which the gods are set to return—would already be in the past. As we know, nothing happened—leaving aside a number of scientifically well-documented UFO sightings.[24] So is it all humbug?

No. The so-called gods of antiquity, those teachers who instructed our Stone Age forefathers in arts such as astronomy, *will* return. I know that only too well; there is too much proof available to leave me in any doubt. We cannot fixate on Sunday, December 23, 2012, though. It's not just the cultures and religions that I've mentioned already that have this belief in the second coming. It pretty much applies to the entire ancient world, from thousands of years ago to the present day.

The Christians are waiting for Jesus to return. You can read about it in the Gospel of Mark (Chapter 13, Verse 26): "And then shall they see the Son of man coming in the clouds with great power and glory."

The Mahdi of the Muslims

It's no different in the Islamic world: The Muslims await the coming of the Mahdi. The Imams—the teachers of Islam—continually reiterate that it is wrong to speculate upon the date of the Mahdi as that is a secret that only Allah may know. Once, a stranger asked the fifth Imam, al-Baqir, what signs would precede the return of the Mahdi. The Imam answered:

> It will be when the women act like men and the men act like women; and when the women sit with spread legs upon saddled horses. It will be when false witnesses are believed and when truth is rejected; then when men spill the blood of other men for no good reason, when they fornicate and squander the money of the poor.[25]

According to these criteria, the Mahdi should have been here long ago. But—the Islamic scholars tell us—before it can happen, 60 false prophets must come. I have no idea how many false prophets there have been, but the number must have exceeded 60 a long time ago.

Islamic literature is totally unclear on when and where this coming will take place. The Mahdi is the redeemer of the final days. He will come "on the twenty-third night of the month of Ramadan."[26] This night "is The Night of Power (Laylat al-Qadr) in which the Qur'an was revealed, the night in which the angels descend."[27]

Judaism is no stranger to this idea, either: Faithful Jews have been waiting for the second coming of their Messiah for more than five thousand years. The Jews, of course, never accepted Jesus as the Messiah.

The concept also crops up in the ancient Iranian Parsee religion. The "Avesta"—it means "basic text" or "teaching"—contains the religious texts of the Parsees, the followers of Zarathustra.[28] Zarathustra himself is said to have been born as a result of an immaculate conception. According to Zoroastrian tradition, a mountain swathed in pure light descended from heaven. A youth emerged from this mountain bearing the embryo of Zarathustra, which he then implanted in his mother's womb. Fragments of this ancient religion are preserved in cuneiform

4.6. Depiction of Ahura Mazda from the Parsee religion. Author's own image.

texts that were made at the order of King Darius the Great (circa 549–486 BC), his son Xerxes (485–465 BC), and his grandson Artaxerxes (464–424 BC). The highest object of worship is the divinity "Ahura Mazda." He is depicted as a ring with wings who reigns over the world. The similarity to the winged sun disks in Egypt can hardly be missed.

All the Gods Are Coming Back!

According to the texts of the Parsees, the constellations are subdivided into star clusters that are ruled by various commanders. Then it gets quite military-sounding, as they talk about the soldiers of the star systems who fight their battles throughout the universe. The *Quadriga solis,* the four-wheeled chariot pulled by winged horses, has its roots in Iranian culture.[29] Here, the gods of the various planets are said to steer the chariot of the sun. In the "Yashts," a kind of subdivsion of the Avesta, you can read in Chapter 10, verses 67 and 68: "Who drives along on his high-wheeled chariot made of a heavenly substance from the Karshvare of Arezahi to the Karshvare of Xwaniratha...white, shining, seen afar, beneficent, endowed with knowledge, swiftly carry along the heavenly space.... (Chapter 10, Verse 125) Four stallions draw that chariot, all of the same white color, living on heavenly food and undying."

Space seems to be full of such flying machines, and the differences between terms like *arrow, bird, heavenly food,* and *made of a heavenly substance* show that the Parsees knew what they were talking about.

Of course, the Parsees too expected their gods to return.[30] "Light beings" would descend from heaven, they believed. Zarathustra himself asked his god Ahura Mazda about the end of time and was told that "all-conquering ones" would come down from the skies. They are immortal; their intellects perfect. Before these divinities appear in the firmament, the sun will go dark, the world will be battered by a mighty storm wind, and a star will fall from heaven. Following a terrible battle, a new dawn will break for humanity. Then mankind will be so well-versed in healing that "even those who are close to death will not die."

The difference here to the redeemers of other religions is not so dramatic at a glance, except for the fact that this time it is the "all-conquerors" who are coming to save the world. These are the ones that the Parsees were waiting for: the gods from the canopy of the stars.

In Hinduism it gets even more complex because of the panoply of gods. Originally, so they believe, the world was free of greed or desires—a place of such happiness that we could scarce imagine it. This enviable paradise survived until negative spirits, but also gods, confused the minds of men. The gods were, admittedly, omnipotent and immortal beings with great power. However, they also displayed a distinctly human nature and had a penchant for taking on human form. The greatest of them all was the Ruler of the Heavens (Indra), who was lord over all.

In *Vanaparvan*—part of the ancient Indian epic Mahabharata (Chapters 168–173)—the gods are said to have lived in veritable space cities that orbited high above the Earth. Here we can say with some certainty that any religious-psychological interpretation is barking up the wrong tree. The following quotes prove it.

In the volume Drona Parva (also a part of the Mahabharata) you can read on page 690, verse 62 how three exquisitely built space cities circled the Earth. What followed was a veritable space battle: "Civa, riding on that excellent car which was composed of all the celestial forces, proceeded for the destruction of the tripple [sic] city.... When, however, the three cities *came together in the firmament*, the lord Mahadeva pierced them with that terrible shaft of his, consisting of three knots." [author's emphasis][31]

The text was translated from the Sanskrit into English in 1888. Nobody back then could have had a clue about intergalactic motherships (that is, cities in the firmament). And anyone who comes up with the objection that "heavenly cities" could simply have been just holy places on Earth will be forced to capitulate in the face of the concrete statement about *three cities in the firmament*. What's more, the destruction of cities "in the firmament" clearly rules out any holy place on Earth. The core of this tale—battles in heaven, wars between the gods—is the decisive factor that leaves the psychologically motivated idea of heaven as represented by the researchers of the old school looking somewhat farcical. Also, the often-repeated objection that mankind has simply always had the need for a "savior" or some other similar "heavenly figure" just doesn't wash in the face of the sheer quantity of documented cases. The messages speak for themselves.

Of course, the Hindus also have their own belief in a second coming: They believe that Vishnu will be born again as Krishna to save the world.

Older Than Buddha

The precursor of Buddhism is the religion of the Jaina, known as Jainism. According to their teachings, the current age is simply one of many (like the Maya and others). Once, they say, so-called *Tirthamkaras* descended from heaven. The first of these was *Rishabha,* and he visited our planet an incredible 8,400,000 years ago.[32] You would expect teachers such as this arriving from outer space to have certain astronomical and astrophysical knowledge. Unsurprisingly perhaps, the Jaina know astronomical data that we do not understand. Their teachings say that dimensions of the universe can be measured. The unit of measurement for this is the *Rajju.* That is the distance that the gods cover in six months when they travel at a speed of 2,057,152 *yojanas* every *samay* (blink of an eye). We have a similar unit of measurement: What, after all, is a light year? It's roughly six trillion miles. According to the Jaina, the entire universe is filled with life that is distributed unevenly around the cosmos. In Jaina thinking, primitive life and plants can be found on all planets that are not too hot or not too cold, but only certain planets can sustain "beings with voluntary movements."[33]

And what about second comings? This is where it really gets good. In a divine realm known as *Kalpas* there are said to be magnificent flying palaces the size of whole cities. These heavenly residences were built like apartment blocks, one floor over the next, so that the "Vimanas" (the heavenly flying machines) would be able to fly out in any direction. Every time a new age begins and a new *Tirthamkaras* is born, a bell rings out in the main palace of the heavenly realm. It is so arranged that this bell triggers bells in all the other 3,199,999 heavenly palaces. Then the gods gather, partially from the love of the *Tirthamkaras* and partially out of curiosity. Those who so desire visit our solar system in a mighty flying palace. And a new age dawns on Earth.

The Same Numbers, but Where Did They Come From?

The Buddhists believe that sometime in the future, the exalted Metteyya (also called Maitreya) will appear on Earth, the perfect Buddha. The Buddhists think in terms of absolutely unbelievable numbers—their so-called "yugas." What is most amazing with these is their consistency with completely separate sources. The number 4,320,000 of the *maha yuga* (the great age) is identical with to of the third antediluvian king *En-men-lu-ana*. He ruled for 12 *sars* (a *sar* is a period of 3,600 years, and 12 × 3,600 = 43,200). You can read this on the Sumerian King List "WB-444" (which is kept today in the British Museum in London). So how does this fit together?

Or let's take the number 288,000 of the *deva yugas*. This corresponds to the number of the sixth ancient king, known as *En-sipad-zid-ana*. He managed to rule for eight *sars*. (That adds up to 28,800 years.) The numbers are the same, give or take the odd zero. In Greece you can find allusions to a so-called "world age" in the works of the poet Heraclitus. He set this number at 10,800,000 years. The same number corresponds to the second period of the Sumerian kings, namely 30 *sars*, or 108,000 years.

This playing around with numbers just goes to show that there is some kind of common denominator running through everything. At some time, back in the mists of time, there must have been something like a standardized source; otherwise all these relationships don't make sense. This common origin must lie way, way back in the dim and distant past. If it were otherwise, the history books would have some mention of it.

In all my contemplation of second comings, the science of psychology doesn't provide me with any clues. There is no basic pattern from out of the psychological pigeonhole that explains these identical numbers or identical attributes—smoke, fire, quaking, noise—described during the descent of the gods, or the artificial inseminations described in the ancient texts. Just for comparison: Catholic Christians believe that Jesus was the result of an immaculate conception. However, the idea of immaculate conceptions is millennia older. Countless major gods and god-kings from ancient times are said to have been conceived immaculately. A lot of this may have been simply self-aggrandizement or narcissism on the part of the royal dynasties. After all, no leader wanted to be seen as anything less than any of his predecessors. The origin of this belief, though, is based on actual events. The gods (= ETs) *did* carry out artificial inseminations. Even the origin of the Egyptian royal dynasty can be traced back to the gods. The ancient historians—those who actually worked thousands of years ago—wrote, without exception, of a race of gods that provided the seed of the first kings. Mankind did not know much about astronomy until they learned it from the gods; as was also the case with the arts of toolmaking and working the soil. Even language and writing systems came courtesy of these helpful heavenly beings: "They were namely the ones who first structured comprehensible language and gave many things names that previously had had none...."[34]

Today's science ignores these reports. They are not seen as helpful; there are too many of them. In the apocrypha, too, there is talk of "heavenly teachers," although here they are referred to as "fallen angels."[35] In the Jewish traditions there are no end of "chosen ones" whose seed was not of earthly origin. It's something that most people would rather sweep under the carpet; they prefer not to dirty their fingers with such concepts. And suddenly Erich von Däniken is associated with idiotic racists, as if the "heavenly seed" were my idea and I had made up the "chosen ones" myself. To make it clear for those who still haven't understood: This entire way of thinking is not the product of my imagination. It comes straight out of those very books that for many people are the holiest of all writings.

Noah, a Child of the ETs

Consequently, Noah, the survivor of the Flood, was not just anybody. Admittedly, his earthly father is given as "Lamech," but Lamech never fathered his son. You can read about this in the Lamech Scroll—one of the famous Dead Sea Scrolls.[36] It tells how Lamech returned home one day from a long journey of several months. Upon entering his tent, he found a young boy who did not seem to be of his family. He had different eyes, a different hair color, and even a different skin color. Furious, Lamech confronted his wife, but she swore by all that is holy to her that she had not been unfaithful, neither with a soldier nor with one of the *sons of God*. Worried, Lamech set off to ask his father for advice. This worthy one was none other than Methuselah himself. He, too, was unable to help and turned to his own father for help, namely Lamech's grandfather. This was Enoch—the seventh antediluvian prophet. Enoch said to his son Methuselah that he should tell Lamech to accept this strange child as if it were his own. The "heavenly beings" had laid their seed in the lap of his wife without sexually abusing her. This young cuckoo was destined to become the progenitor of a new race after the Flood. Lamech was to call the lad Noah. And he did.

What does this delightful story have to do with the return of the gods? This episode shows that Enoch—Lamech's grandfather!—already knew about the coming flood catastrophe. In other words, the Flood was no natural catastrophe, it was planned. And the "Most High" (the starship captain) who had had Enoch "kidnapped" told him this personally.[37] Who arranged the artificial insemination of Lamech's wife? The same space travelers who also instructed Enoch in several branches of science and carried him away from the Earth in a "fiery chariot." Enoch is another one who, after a long absence, is expected to "return to the Earth."[38]

Gesar Came From the Heavens, Too

In his flawlessly documented book on ancient Tibet, Willi Grömlin proves that the original Tibetan kings were extraterrestrial in origin.[39] Gesar was one such: He possessed a flying machine that mightily impressed his people and even brought an alien object with him down to Earth: the "dorje." It was a kind of multipurpose weapon. Models of it can be seen in Tibetan temples. These aliens also brought indecipherable writings with them from the skies. Some of these remain hidden in a cave "for the future generations who are capable of understanding them."[40] The original kings of Tibet came from outer space. Some of them returned there later—with the promise that they would return sometime in the distant future. What else?

4.7. Model of a dorje in front of a Tibetan temple. Author's own image.

We've strayed from the point somewhat. We were actually talking about the return of the gods of the Mayan world. But the Maya weren't alone in their beliefs, whether they knew it or not. The expectation that the gods will return remains an irrevocable fact. Worldwide. Christians and Jews await their Messiah, and Muslims the Mahdi, merely another word for a messianic figure. A normal person who later becomes a king cannot be a Messiah, for the simple reason that the word *man* (or *human* or *person*) is totally inappropriate for explaining the Messiah. Professor Hugo Gressmann, a recognized exegete for the Old Testament, analyzes it thus: "For both to be the same thing seems to be more than unlikely, for the Messiah appears to be a heavenly being. What is more, he is also considered to be pre-existent. He existed before humans were even around."[41]

Clearly, not all religions can be right. Some of them must be barking up the wrong tree, mustn't they? But what if *all of them* are wrong? The motif of returning gods belongs no more to the Maya, than it does to the Inca people, the Egyptians, the Buddhists, the Christians, the Muslims, the Jews, or anyone else on this Earth. This expectation of some kind of return is global and harks back to a promise given by the extraterrestrials to our forefathers thousands of years ago. "We'll be back!" they said to some of their students. The Maya have preserved this promise literally and even give a date for it: December 23, 2012. If our calendar is right, then this is a date that we could pretty much rely on.

They're Coming Back!

You can be absolutely certain that those ETs—or their descendants—will be making another visit to our planet. It can be proved. So it's all the more inexplicable to me why this simple truth triggers such a clamorous reaction in our society—why ethnologists reject it so indignantly. The denial practiced by organized religions is no great surprise. The exegetic interpretations so far have just produced greater confusion. They have—and this in no way diminishes my great respect for the industrious work by the translators of the ancient texts—simply led to nothing. What's more, the plethora of contradictions will continue to exist because the starting premises are false. *Quetzal serpent* is just one term in a litany of thousands that are and will remain meaningless as long as the science of psychology insists on talking even the banalest things to pieces. In my book *Der Götterschock* (*The God Shock*), I believe I have painted a pretty clear and, most importantly, well-founded picture of how our forefathers came to see the "divine" in technical devices. The feedback I've received from my worldwide readership shows that they have certainly understood. The only problem is that the scientists in charge insist on understanding nothing. Their prejudices and preconceptions cloud their judgment so much that none of them would ever dare to support my theories in public.

It's not only the so-called gods who will be returning, though: To support themselves, those beings from outer space will also reactivate the many objects and texts that have been deposited on the Earth—deposited millennia ago for just this purpose. Those legendary teachers did not just pack up all their belongings when they rocketed off into the beyond; looking ahead to the distant future, they left behind many things in indestructible storage depots. But why should they do something so seemingly banal—something so "human"? So they would have proof in the future: that they (or their forefathers) had been here before many thousands of years ago. And that they had left such objects behind. *Where?* In a cave in Tibet those very gods deposited texts and objects for use in the future. These are described by Willi Grömling from page 263 onward in his book.[42] In Egypt, in the hidden rooms under the Great Pyramid and the Sphinx, as well as under the "Osirion" in Abydos. And finally, in Ecuador in South America at the coordinates 77°47'34" west and 1°56'00" south. This is the location of a library of metal panels stored deliberately for the future. By whom? By those very aliens who made it into the Book of Mormon. Admittedly, this is a religious work just like the Bible, but the Book of Mormon starts by describing events in ancient times. Just like in the Bible. Here are a couple of passages from Chapter 8, 16 ff. (The numbers in parentheses correspond to the numbering in the Book of Mormon.)

> And blessed be he that shall bring this thing to light; for it shall be brought out of darkness unto light, according to the word of God; yea, it shall be brought out of the earth, and it shall shine forth out of darkness, and come unto the knowledge of the people...(26)... and none can stay it; and it [the texts] shall come in a day when it shall be said that miracles are done away; and it shall come even as if one should speak from the dead.... (29) ...Yea, it shall come in a day when there shall be heard of fires, and tempests, and vapors of smoke in foreign lands.... (30) ...And there shall also be heard of wars, rumors of wars, and earthquakes in divers places.[43]

And if anyone thinks, "A-ha! Däniken is a Mormon!" Well, they can think again. I am indeed a spiritual and religious man, fully convinced of the creation at the hands of the "Great Spirit of Creation," as I think of the unfathomable one, but I certainly do not belong to any church or religious grouping.

The Legacies

There's something wrong with our past. That's a conclusion that is 100-percent certain and even attestable. There are ancient texts, like the book of the "prophet" Enoch, who learned the language of the extraterrestrials, quotes their names, and finally disappears into the firmament in a fiery chariot with the vague promise that he will, one day, return to good old Earth. (I wrote extensively on this subject in my last book, *History Is Wrong.*) There is Manetho, the hardworking chronicler in ancient Egypt whose lists include 380 kings with names and dates that modern Egyptology wants nothing to do with.[44] Or there's the church father Eusebius[45] who, just like Herodotus[46] and his historian colleague Diodorus[47], listed the dates of bygone leaders that make contemporary archaeologists cringe. We are certainly not on the right path as far as ancient human history is concerned. We ought to be proud of the fact that extraterrestrial "gods" instructed our forefathers.

Instead, archaeologists and other "-ologists" are too busy fighting over the correct interpretation of ancient written records. (Is there anything we humans don't fight over?) Herodotus and company are accused of erring and even lying because—let's face it—contemporary knowledge is the culmination of all our experience from the past to the present. But how can that be when we ignore the wisdom of the early historians? Our current knowledge is the be all and end all? Hogwash! We spurn not only the ancient observers, but also the visible, tangible, photographable, rock-hard evidence right under our noses. Underneath the temple of Sethos I in Abydos (Egypt) lies an extremely impressive megalithic puzzle—something that every tourist can see and something that is clearly very much older than the Sethos temple itself. Does anybody care? Daniel Ruzo, former lawyer and Jesuit student in Peru, presented a series of stone monuments that all clearly had their origins in an unknown prehistoric age.[48] No branch of science felt that this had anything to do with them. There is practically never any money available for financing research. The same is the case for the inexplicable high plateau "El Enladrillado" in Chile. This lies in the province of Talca, around 37 miles to the east of the town of Talca and not far from "Altos de Vilches" (roughly 35°37' south, 71°05' west). At an altitude of around 6,500 feet lie hundreds of stone blocks, all perfectly cut and furrowed—clearly an artificial construction. But from whom? Whoever it was lived in a time earlier than any known culture in Chile. Therefore they don't fit into our evolutionary pattern—just like Puma Punku in the highlands of Bolivia. Homberto Sarnataro Bounaud, the leader of a small expedition to El Enladrillado in fall 1968, noted: "There is no doubt that a previous ancient culture once lived here. The indigenous people of this zone would never have been capable of constructing anything on this scale."[49]

In 2008, the young Chilean teacher Rafael Eissmann visited the mysterious plateau. He put together an extremely well-documented and well-researched publication on the mysterious El Enladrillado[50] and told me personally, "There is certainly something not right here. No tribe has lived on this plateau for thousands of years. If they had done, the Chilean archaeologists would know about it. So these cut blocks must have been put here by some really ancient culture."

4.8. The stone slabs of El Enladrillado, in Chile. Public domain image.

The picture above proves what he says. Which science or which research foundation is going to pick up the ball and run with this?

In Chapter 1 I told you about the heavyweight platforms in Puma Punku, Bolivia. I showed you pictures of the perfectly cut blocks with the millimeter-wide grooves that *couldn't possibly* have been made with Stone Age tools, or have been the result of Stone Age planning talents—certainly not in any culture that we know of. I showed you the precise calendar calculations carried out by Dr. Edmund Kiss. You can flip back and take another look if you like; in fact I recommend you do. Kiss's year was 12 months of 24 days, with each day being made up of 30 hours, which were 22 minutes long. This calendar agrees exactly with the Mayan calendar and, what's more, reaches 10,000 years back into the past. Is anyone anywhere getting excited about it? Is anyone jumping up in excitement about these millimeter-precise calculations? Is there any chief editor crying out, "Man, that's just unbelievable!" before going out to drum up money for research projects?

Society has become sluggish and lazy, overfed by the Internet, and crushed by a zeitgeist that immediately stifles any enthusiasm—too lazy to take notice of anything important or groundbreaking.

Our attitude toward these old truths will have no influence on the return of the "gods." They'll be back, and their mere presence will shake our self-satisfied souls to the core. December 23, 2012: that is the date from the Maya calendar. Even if this date is not the one, the god shock will still come. You can bet your life on it.

CHAPTER 5

THE ETERNAL INTELLIGENCE

Two hundred and fifty years ago philosopher Immanuel Kant wrote in his *Critique of Pure Reason*: "I should not hesitate to stake my all on the truth of the proposition...that, at least, some one of the planets, which we see, is inhabited."[1]

Apart from the odd UFO sighting and alleged contacts with UFO crews—which, as of yet, have not been scientifically verified—there has been no contact during our modern age with "inhabitants" from other planets. So do they even exist? As early as 1950, world-famous nuclear physicist Enrico Fermi asked: "If a multitude of extraterrestrial civilizations exist out there, where are they?"[2] Good question: Where are they? The question soon became famous the world over; it is now known as the "Fermi paradox."

In the English-speaking world there is no shortage of highly scientific publications that are either pro or con on the subject of extraterrestrials. With ice-cold objectivity they deal with questions that leave people in other parts of the world shaking their heads. You can only join in if you speak good English. It's no great surprise to me that there is no funding for ET research in the non-English-speaking parts of Europe. Maybe the English speakers are better informed, or maybe they're just more open to such things.

The Fermi Paradox

Scientist William Hosek gave his opinion on the Fermi paradox in the specialist journal *JBIS* (*Journal of the British Interplanetary Society*). And what was his scientifically based conclusion? "Consequently humans have not, and will not, be visited by them and humans will not visit other civilizations."[3] What makes him so sure?

Hosek looks at the Fermi paradox from a purely economic point of view. He assumes—and he's almost certainly right—that on every inhabited planet the available raw materials will all get used up eventually. People, however, are not created to be long-range planners. That is to say, they don't really think beyond the span of their own lives—that is, in terms of centuries. Regardless of whether we're talking about the public or private sector, whether states or multinational companies, investments are never made with future centuries in mind, because people expect to see some kind of return (for their stakeholders, or in time for the next election, and so on). If man ever sent a starship out to seek raw materials, those left behind would never know if the ship's crew were going to be successful or come back empty-handed. Can you imagine any institution investing maybe billions of dollars in a project with no guarantee of any return? People don't live for very long, and they want to see results. Not only that: Building a gigantic generation starship (a spaceship designed for journeys longer than the lifespan of its crew) would not only cost huge amounts of money, but would itself also require great quantities of precious raw materials—just those materials, in fact, that the home planet is running short on. Logically, such raw materials cannot be risked on an incredibly expensive space adventure that won't bear fruit until hundreds of years later—if at all.

Hosek applies this "earthly" logic to extrasolar civilizations too. And the results of his analysis are quite sobering: *First,* before we receive any help from an alien civilization, we would need to know the "strangers" and at least be in regular radio contact with them. *Second,* the alien civilization would need to be more advanced than ours. *Third,* any civilization would need to be in a position to receive our messages, translate them, and finally understand them. *Fourth,* they would have to be able to provide the raw materials that we are looking for. *Fifth,* they would have to be willing to share their technology and raw materials with us. *Sixth,* we would have to capable of making use of their tools and instructions. And *finally,* the ETs out there would inevitably also be aware that their own raw materials are going to run out, too, sometime. Therefore it hardly seems likely that any alien civilization is going to present its valuable raw materials to any other civilization.

All of this sounds fairly plausible—from an economic point of view. Dr. William R. Hosek, the author of this scientific article, states quite specifically that his observations are purely economic assumptions. So we can forget future space travel because we humans want to see short-term results and simply do not have the resources to build a gigantic starship. (I'll come back to this later.)

SETI

What about radio contact? Aren't we always reading stuff about some SETI project? SETI stands for Search for Extraterrestrial Intelligence.) Aren't millions of dollars being spent every year on huge radio telescopes so that we can receive and send signals? Didn't we already send signals into space in 1960 as part of 'Project Ozma'? Is it possible that some alien answer came long ago and is being kept secret so as to avoid mass panic among the peoples of the world?

Well, the answers to all these questions are a lot more complex than they might seem at first glance. We don't know the precise wavelengths at which interstellar communication operates. The Ozma project in 1960 was carried out by a group of leading scientists in Green Bank, West Virginia. Back then, they opted for a wavelength of 21 centimeters (8.3 inches), which corresponds to the neutral element hydrogen. Seeing as hydrogen is present throughout the entire universe, they believed that extraterrestrial civilizations would use this wavelength to communicate on. Today, we're a bit smarter than that. The 21-centimeter wavelength is extremely susceptible to interference. Out there in space—which we once presumed was completely empty—it hisses, bubbles, bangs, beeps and crackles the whole time. There's a whole soup of noises that need to be filtered out before you could hear anything. Even before that happens, you would have to fathom out whether the signal even originates from an "intelligent" source or whether it's just one of those many sources of interference. Despite all these efforts, to this day not one single radio signal has arrived from an intelligent species. The question has to be: Should we send out signals? Should we be the ones to stand up and shout into space: Hello! It's us! Is it even possible? And how much energy would we have to use to even have a chance of being heard by someone out there?

Professor George Swenson of the University of Illinois has devoted himself to this problem. Swenson is a former astronomer and an engineer. His specialties were electrical oscillations and antenna construction. Writing in the scientific journal *Scientific American,* Swenson analyzed the immense difficulties associated with radio astronomy.[4] Should we direct our signals at some specific target out there in space? Home in on a particular planet? To be able to do that, we would have to know the location of a planet that is home to an intelligent species. The extraterrestrials living there would have to be ready to receive signals, have receiver antennas installed, and use a technology that was at least similar to ours. Added to this, planets do not only rotate around their own axis, but also along an elliptical orbit around their sun. How would it be possible to aim for an exact point in space from here on Earth? This is a point, let's not forget, that is several light years away from Earth and, to be honest, we can't really know if it even exists!

So we've ruled out choosing an exact point and we decide to send out a broad signal. After all, a normal radio antenna here on Earth doesn't send its signal direct to the recipient, but rather sends out its signal in all directions. It is available to all recipients at the same time. In radio astronomy this is known as "omnidirectional" (in other words, present throughout the broadcasting sector). But there's no way we could send out a signal to the entire Milky Way; the energy that would be necessary would not be available anywhere—except perhaps from a nearby neutron star. That means, then, that we would have to concentrate on a selected sector of the Milky Way. There are just two stars within five light years of our solar system; within 10 light years this number jumps to 12. Increase the circle to 15 light years and we have 39 stars, and within 50 light years as many as a hundred. Within a hundred light years the number of stars multiplies a thousandfold. Nowadays, we know that many of these stars have their own planets. What we don't know is whether any of these planets have Earth-like conditions or whether they can support any intelligent life. How powerful would our terrestrial transmitter have to be to send out an omnidirectional signal over a distance of 100 light years?

Professor Swenson took the trouble to work this out. In his words, the transmitter would have to have "more than 7,000 times the total electricity-generating capacity of the U.S."[5] Even using nuclear energy, that's simply not possible. What remains is the approach we have always used: to shine our little light into the darkness and hope that someone out there sees it—or that one of our receiving stations (which are technically highly developed and extremely sensitive) will some day be lucky enough to pick up some stray signal from an extraterrestrial source.

There *Are* Answers

Does that put an end to every discussion on interstellar travel or radio contact with ETs? It certainly doesn't, praise the creator! The opinions of one group—however objective and rational they may be—will always conflict with those of another group that is equally as objective and rational. And we shouldn't forget that, according to Professor Robert Haviland of Daytona Beach, Florida: "The space program is being pushed ahead for now by amateurs who have already described every aspect of interstellar travel and space research. Even the theory of relativity...was developed by an amateur, a secretary in a Swiss patent office, without any backing from the state or any university."[6]

Einstein (that very patent clerk) held to the maxim that "if there is a solution to this problem, then I will find it."[7] Problems have always existed; you can find them everywhere and—depending on the current state of knowledge—many of those who consider themselves to be "rational" happily declaim, "Impossible!" Others, on the other hand, start looking for solutions. This is no coincidence. In the depths of our subconscious—call it our soul, if you will—we realize that their is a solution somewhere for every "impossibility." It's down to the "memes" or "universal consciousness" that I mentioned briefly in Chapter 1. (More about this later.)

Warp Drives?

In November 2007, the British Interplanetary Society organized a symposium in London on the subject of the warp drive. This is a theoretical propulsion unit that would allow faster-than-light travel. The basic mathematical framework for the warp drive was worked out as early as 1994. Warp speed is reached by bending (or "warping") the space-time continuum. These "curvatures in space" were predicted by Einstein; now their existence has been proven. (Huge heavenly bodies bend light, for instance.) At the London symposium a number of "rational" mathematicians and astrophysicists talked about the expansion of the universe, about gravitational fields in the vacuum of space, and about the possibility of leaping from one "bubble" to another without losing time.[8] The warp drive, the scientists agreed, would exploit our knowledge of mass, space-time, and quantum physics without contravening any of the fundamental laws of physics.[9]

Laymen may scratch their heads and cry, "Impossible!" But the fact that nothing is impossible is even alluded to by the God of the Old Testament: "This is only the start of what they may do: and now it will not be possible to keep them from any purpose of theirs" (Genesis 11:6).

As early as 1984, Professor Michael Papagiannis, an astronomer at Boston University, postulated that the proliferation of a species within our Milky Way could be possible. And all this without any "warp drive," which wasn't even a subject of discussion back then. According to Papagiannis: "At a velocity of 2 percent of light speed, which is possible with the help of nuclear fusion, a spaceship will cover a distance of ten light years in about 500 years."[10]

After this, the space colonists would need around another 500 years to industrialize a planet. That's quite plausible. After all, we needed just 200 hundred years to progress from horse-drawn carriages to moon rockets, and from the abacus to the super-computer—and we had to invent everything from scratch. Our theoretical interstellar colonists wouldn't have to start from point "zero," because all the plans and fabrication methods would already be available to them. The space travelers would not need to discover how to extract raw materials from the earth, smelt steel, produce plastics, or generate electricity. After a stop of 500 years, they could move on—either using the old mother ship, or in a new one of their own construction. Again they would be in transit for 500 years, and so on. Papagiannis noted: "This means that each wave of colonization takes 1,000 years to cover roughly 10 light years (500 years traveling and 500 years of establishment and growth). That corresponds to a speed of one light year per century."[11]

Colonies in Space

In other words, we could colonize the entire Milky Way in 10 million years, and the only "expense" would be the initial starship. All of this without any warp drive.

Since Papagiannis made these claims in 1983, his calculations have been updated several times. Astronomer Ian Crawford from University College in London suggests a proliferation rate of 10 percent of light speed and a period of 400 years between setting up a new colony and the next phase: "In this way, the wave of colonization moves on at a rate of 0.02 light years per year. Seeing as the Milky Way has a diameter of approximately 100,000 light years, it will take around five million years to completely colonize it."[12]

Five million years corresponds to just 0.05 percent of the age of the Milky Way. Are we human beings ourselves offshoots of an extraterrestrial colony without even knowing it? "Impossible!" cry the evolutionists. (How many times is that now?) It can be demonstrated conclusively that we evolved on the Earth. No contradiction, answer the problem solvers. The human race can have arisen on the Earth via the usual evolutionary routes—absolutely. But, sometime over the course of the last few thousands years, there was a targeted, artificial mutation introduced by just those ETs that are worshipped as "gods"—as was recorded in the ancient texts. This doesn't contradict evolution—rather it complements it with the creation of a (symbolic) Adam and Eve. But there are other ways of looking at it.

Just imagine that you are sitting in an airplane that is spiraling around the Earth. The aircraft is packed full with the seeds of oak trees. Every hour you open the window and throw out a handful of seeds. Of course, you realize that a large portion of the seeds will be lost in the oceans. (After all, two thirds of the Earth's surface is covered in water.) Some of them will land on sand—deserts such as Sahara, Nevada, Gobi, or Baluchistan. Yet more land on stone, and others land somewhere in the ice of the Arctic or Antarctic. Only a small proportion of the seeds that are scattered have a chance of landing on suitable terrain and *then* not being eaten by some rodent. That small proportion soon begins to sprout, though, and finally you have a fully grown oak tree. Maybe it will have a few mutations, but it will still be ostensibly an oak tree, because the important genetic information is already contained in the seed.

Panspermia Explains It All!

Now transfer this model to the entire universe. The idea comes from the Swedish Nobel prize–winner Savante Arrhenius (1859–1927). Arrhenius was a professor of physics at the University of Stockholm and was way ahead of his time. Somewhere, way out there in the universe—so Arrhenius theorized—the very first intelligences began to develop a long, long time ago. (The question as to how this first life form arose is as unanswerable as the question "how long is a piece of string?") This first intelligent race—let's call it Number 1—was interested in proliferating its own species throughout the universe. There are plenty of reasons for this. Just like a virus, Number 1 sends out billions upon billions of its own germ seeds out into the cosmos—just as randomly as our seeds from the airplane. Number 1 knows that the majority of its building blocks for life will end up burning up in a sun, rain down on an unsuitable planet, or end up coming to naught for some other reason. Some of these building blocks will clatter down onto planets that are similar to Number 1's home planet. Thus sprouts the seed of life and, soon after, the evolution process kicks in.

In science, this theory is known as panspermia and is one logical explanation of how intelligence may spread throughout the universe—without a warp drive, without any faster-than-light speeds, and without any colonies sent out on generation starships.

Building Blocks From "Out There"

The origin of life on Earth is truly a puzzle and cannot be simply explained by the existence of a "primeval soup" or some "niche hypothesis." I have spent the last 30 years writing about the subject.[13] In that period more than 600 scientific publications have been published on the subject of the origin of life and the general tenor is always the same. What we ought to remember is that "evolution" and the "origin of life" really should be treated separately. Evolution is the biological transformation of species (Darwin). The origin of life, on the other hand, happens *before* evolution. This is all about chemical building blocks and the physics behind it.

Professor Bruno Vollmert, a macrobiologist and former director of the Polymer Institute at the University of Karlsruhe, Germany, notes: "Seeing as the macromolecular preconditions are not fulfilled, the Neo-Darwinism prevalent today is untenable as a scientific hypothesis."[14]

Sir Fred Hoyle, for many years professor of astronomy and astrophysics at the University of Cambridge, is of the same opinion:

> In pre-Copernican times, the Earth was wrongly considered to be the geometric and physical center of the universe. These days, even respectable scientists still regard the Earth as the biological center of the universe. An almost unbelievable repetition of the same earlier mistake.... The only possible explanation for evolution is if the genetic material (necessary for the origin of life) came from somewhere outside of our system, in other words from somewhere completely different.[15]

Together with mathematical genius Professor Wickramasinghe from Cardiff University, Wales, Sir Fred Hoyle published a book called *Lifecloud: The Origin of Life in the Universe*. The two academics' findings can be summed up in the following statement: "There was never any home development stage here on Earth. Life had already developed to a relatively high information content before the Earth was even there. By the time we received life, all of the basic biological questions had already been answered."[16]

It goes on like this; I know the treatises. Even the dyed-in-the-wool supporters of the birth of life on Earth, like Dr. David Horn, professor of anthropology at Colorado State University, admit today that my books have given them serious cause for thought. Even Professor Horn now agrees: "Life arrived here from outer space."[17]

Why do we keep twisting and turning, and trying to reject this sensible and scientifically provable standpoint? The thought that we are not the "apotheosis of creation" or the "pinnacle of evolution" really goes against the grain for some people. We like to think of ourselves as the best thing in the galaxy—pure egocentricity, I'd like to add. The Earth was never a closed system. We were and still are unequivocally bound to the universe—a fact, by the way, that is an intrinsic part of many of our holy books: "And God made man in his image." (Genesis 27). But what do we care about holy books?

The Church and ETs

In the year 1600, Domincan monk Giordano Bruno was burned at the stake for uttering the "monstrous idea that intelligent life may exist elsewhere in the universe. 400 years later the pontifical culture commission declared this execution to be unlawful."[18]

The Catholic Church has fundamentally changed its stance and it's mainly down to two Jesuits: Pierre Teilhard de Chardin (1881–1955) and José Gabriel Funes (1963–). The latter is an Argentinean and has been the director of the Vatican Observatory "Specolo Vaticana" since August 2006. A total of 12 Jesuits—I call them the "papal guard of intelligence"—look after the telescopes and the Zeiss astrographs on the roof of Castel Gandolfo. The Jesuits were always the forward thinkers of the Catholic church. They make sure that the Roman Curia doesn't get stuck in the Middle Ages and also do their bit to ensure that the fame of the Jesuits extends beyond the Earth. As a result, 30 lunar craters carry the name of Jesuit astronomers.

Foremost among these forward thinkers was philosopher and Jesuit priest Pierre Teilhard de Chardin. He recognized that there was a clear link between man and the cosmos. The fundamental building block of matter is the atom, and that applies all throughout the universe. Atoms themselves consist of a nucleus and subatomic particles, and they are not simply "there"; they are subject to vibrations. Elementary particles—I mentioned this in Chapter 1—did not acquire their strange and baffling characteristics from nowhere, but from their interaction with other particles. The word itself says it: A *particle* is a "part" of something else, and the whole is reflected in every constituent particle. Teilhard de Chardin was already talking about this back in 1949. His term *aleph* covers everything, the alpha and the omega, and this includes cause and effect.[19] Even his Jesuit brethren found Teilhard de Chardin a little bit uncanny. In 1962, seven years after his death, the Catholic Church decided—following years of hefty theological arguments—that

Teilhard's views contradicted Christian teachings. As astrophysicists today now know, however, Teilhard de Chardin was perfectly right, just like Giordano Bruno all those centuries previously.

José Gabriel Fuentes, director of the Vatican Observatory, no longer has to struggle against such antiquated and outdated opinions. In an interview in the Vatican journal *L'Osservatore Romano,* he was asked his opinion on the possibility of extraterrestrial life. His answer:

> In the same way that there are a large number of creatures on the Earth, there could also be other life forms—even intelligent ones— that were also created by God. This does not conflict with our faith, because we may not set limits on God's creative freedom. As St. Francis might say: If we look at the earthly creations as "brothers" and "sisters," why can't we also talk about an "extraterrestrial brother"? He would, after all, also be a part of creation.[20]

Required Forms

Evolution is truly a buzzword of our times. Down here on Earth it is at least—with a few exceptions—demonstrable. But evolution is also universal. We are just a microscopic side show in cosmic evolution. This evolution has required forms—whether it's here on Earth or anyplace else, and whether on a minute scale or a massive scale. Required forms on a small scale can be things like the fact that the brain of any intelligent species is always in the immediate vicinity of the eyes, for example. It has to be like that, because this is the quickest route for the neurons. As soon as the eye sees something, the brain reacts. Or, every nose, proboscis, trunk, or other olfactory organ is located not far from the mouth—you need to smell something before you eat it. Of the grasping tools—arms, hands, tentacles, and so forth—at least one is always aligned to the front. After all, you need to see what what you touch. We humans all believe that we've got something that we call free will. It's true, when it comes to trivial, everyday things—but not when it comes to anything important. Just try to do anything to stop curiosity!

Let's say, for the sake of argument, that dolphins are highly intelligent life forms. At night, while jumping out of the water, they observe small lights in varying degrees of brightness and different colors twinkling in the firmament. The dolphin council swims together to discuss the question: Is there anything out there? Are there other kinds of dolphins maybe? Sooner or later—in evolutionary terms it's not so important when—the dolphins decide to attempt interstellar travel to find the answer to this burning question. space travel is not possible to a non-metallic culture. To blend and cast metals, you need fire. To make fire, you need to get out of the water! Required forms!

Evolution, mutation, and selection are everyday occurrences in the universe. Solar systems and planetary systems are formed. Some of them are well suited for the transportation of panspermia; others are not so ideal (selection). Astrophysicists ask themselves: What happened before the Big Bang? Practically all of them use the concept of a "singularity"—which was the state *before* the Big Bang happened, around 14 billion years ago. But where did this singularity come from? Something appearing from nothing—that's certainly anything but scientific. One solution for this dilemma is "loop quantum gravity," or LQV. According to this theory, space consists of "space quanta," which are comparable to the little hills you might find on a ski piste. The skier doesn't bash his way through these; he has to adjust to them. Just like time. Quantum gravitation theory precludes the existence of so-called "worm holes" in space: "...spacetime does not consist of strings or atoms of spacetime, but a region of infinite boredom: the structure found just below the threshold will simply repeat itself on every smaller scale, ad infinitum...."[21]

We Joe Publics can't really picture it. After all, space quanta measure just one "Planck length." That's something like a billionth of a trillionth of a centimeter.

The important thing is to realize that this loop quantum gravitation can be used to "get around" the singularity (the nothing before the Big Bang). The result is no longer a Big Bang, but rather a "big bounce." Another universe existed *before* our Big Bang. Our big bang was, in fact, the death knell of a previous universe. And so it goes on for eternity.

It stills begs the question, of course: When did this all start? That's one that nobody's going to be able to answer in a hurry. We're getting closer to the vibrations—the oscillations that can be found in all matter. I would like to take the liberty to call these fundamental vibrations the "Great Spirit of Creation." Others might use the word "God."

Omnipresent Memes

The proliferation of vibrations and matter throughout the universe can be proven and with them the existence of "memes." Two things shape us: The "gene" is a fundamental biological component. We originated and still function on a genetic basis. The "meme," on the other hand, influences our consciousness. It is present everywhere and at every possible time—past present, and future—and acts in a similar fashion to a virus. (A virus is not a true life form, by the way it needs another life form to reproduce.) Memes, too, are not life forms. They need our brains to propagate them. This functions, curiously enough, according to the same selection process as in evolution. Let me illustrate this with an example.

You, my dear reader, are reading this book. The ideas in it may excite you; you may agree with them or disagree. Let's just say, for the sake of argument, that you are an enthusiastic recipient of the content of this book and you recommend it to others. They are "infected" by your thought processes, read the book themselves, and encourage others to read it. A wave of approval for the book spreads out. Or we go the other way, and spread negative propaganda. This in turn causes people *not* to buy the book, and our little wave is stopped in its tracks. A kind of natural selection has taken place.

This happens every day in our society. A rumor spreads or dies out; the same applies to jokes or information. Either it takes hold—in other words it is considered interesting, clever, or important—or it dissolves into nothing. What is "interesting" can also be the start signal for further research, which, in itself, can be the starting point for yet more investigations. Examples include human knowledge about astronomy from the Stone Age to the present day, and mathematics from counting on fingers to the supercomputer. Memes multiply, but only when it's worth the effort (selection again). The information must be interesting and important, fascinating, and stimulating. Only then, when all minds are infected, does the world of scientific research really kick into gear. The driving force is curiosity, that beast that never stops asking questions. The proliferation of memes—the multiplication of thoughts—brings every intelligent species inevitably to a stage where it begins researching the realm of space. Why? Because at some time, most of the questions regarding earthly matters have been answered. Then all eyes turn away from the Earth and toward the next dimension. It's a compulsion!

Anyone who argues that the proliferation of information within human society is the most normal thing in the world and we don't need any "memes" to achieve this most likely hasn't got a clue what these vibrations are capable of. Animals that find food at a certain location share this information with their fellows via a kind of thought transferral process. Are these memes? It has been clearly demonstrated among various species of birds, such as crows and vultures.[22]

The information in the gray cells in our skulls is networked and transmitted via electrical impulses. These in themselves are vibrations. What they lead to is "consciousness." Consciousness is just as unmeasurable as phenomena like love—but it exists and it vibrates. Anyone who has ever fallen in love knows that the feeling persists even when his or her partner is not there. So it's not just simply about chemical responses in the body; it's about what *causes* those chemical reactions in the first place. The chemicals in the body—the chains of molecules—do not just start reacting without reason. Without information from the eyes, the taste organs, the emotions, and, at the end of the response chain, the brain, sex hormones won't even be sent out on their journey around the body. The electrons within us (subatomic particles) vibrate at a rate of 10 to the power 23 times per second—it's been measured—and give off information in the process.[23] How does that work? In the same way that atoms take on energy (that is, via minuscule vibrations caused by electrical energy), the electron leaves its "mother atom" quick as a flash and jumps into a nearby atom. Because the charge of an atom always has to remain constant, though, in the very same billionth of a second, an electron from this neighboring atom jumps into the gap left by the first electron following its "escape." The two electrons race toward each other—without ever touching—and then part as each electron takes up the vacant position left by its fellow, orbiting around the atomic nucleus. This is because electrons repel each other. Each electron is driven by a power that, at the same time, keeps it apart from all the others. In passing, though, the electrons exchange information! How does that happen? "Black photons" (massless light quanta with extremely short wavelengths) exchange radiation with the black photons of other electrons. This can be measured by the so-called "Schwarzschild radiation," named after astronomer Karl Schwarzschild (1873–1916).

The important thing during these thought processes is the fact that the electron is "immortal" (unlike other particles that puff out into nothingness after a short time). The electron has always been a stable particle; it has existed since the creation of the universe. Electrons penetrated (and still penetrate) the Earth, every stone, every plant— and everything carries some kind of information. Bodies die and decay, the electron lives on and transports endless knowledge in relays from the past into the future—and vice versa. Wow! How? Just like in a black hole, electron time also runs backward. The electron "knows" events that lie far in the future or deep in the past.

The Electron Was Always There

French nuclear physicist Jean Charon said of the electron's amazing properties:

> All matter used in the building of a living or thinking structure and which possessed its qualities of consciousness during that structure's relatively short lifespan, cannot simply return to its original, diffuse minimal state after the structure has died. Information, once collected, can never again be lost; no power in the world can ever cause the regression of an elementary particle consciousness after the death of a complex organized structure.[24]

The Big Bang that kick-started our universe already contained the entire gamut of vibrations (information) from the previous universe (from its final Big Bang). Matter—which is comprised solely of atoms and their subatomic particles—arose from these vibrations. This included the electrons that jump untiringly from one atom to the next collecting information and moving on. We live in an iridescent world of vibrations. The entire universe is filled with these vibrations— and we are part of all this. As thinking and acting beings, we create vibrations in matter. We think it is possible to build a house, and we build one. Thoughts become matter. We ponder about the feasibility and rationality of space travel, and then we develop plans for a starship. We are the "doers"; we implement the vibrations.

A tree or a head of lettuce is no more in a position to do this than a crocodile or an anteater. They, like any piece of hard rock, are made of just the same original matter—atoms and their electrons. Vibrations, though, are in a position to develop reason, deductive capabilities, and consciousness, and the ability to form matter in a conscious, targeted manner (hands, tools, machines, and so forth). They will do it first out of a desire for comfort (houses, clothing, washing machines, vehicles) and then for knowledge. Knowledge wants to expand; curiosity knows no rest; and every intelligence wants to go out into space. Knowledge wants to spread and multiply. (The poor lettuce, on the other hand, has no organs of implementation with which it could pass on the knowledge inherent in its electrons.)

The memes act like viruses that infect us. They are a kind of information medium that flashes messages from one brain to another. They infect the brains of other beings and are filed away for later use. Then they can be called up when necessary or possibly to infect other brains—a fascinating method of self-propagation.

I am neither an esoteric nor a fan of those sensitive people known as "mediums" who are always telling us that they are able to contact another plane of existence. Maybe I should pay more attention to them and find out a bit more about the world of mediums. My reasoning intellect resists, however, for the simple reason that I always look for material evidence and my life is just too short for me to start traveling completely new paths. My subconscious, on the other hand, knows that nothing is impossible—even those things that (honest and genuine) mediums want to tell me. Dr. Heinke Sudhoff is one such medium who claims she can tap the "spirit of the universe." The result is a series of insights such as these: "In the beginning—before consciousness— there was just spirit...the spirit of the great one...there was no space and no time...just emptiness...in which all forms existed as possibilities, in which everything was laid out as vibrations and energy...."[25]

Dr. Sudhoff claims to have received this message from the vibrations of the universe. Is she a theoretical physicist with a deep knowledge of subatomic particles and the properties of electrons? Not at all. She studied archaeology and English, and knows as much about theoretical physics as any other layperson. There is, she writes, something like a "holotropic state of consciousness" in which one can experience the "unity of the universe as an indivisible whole."[26] And she talks of a "state of bliss,"[27] which I personally have also experienced (let me assure you here, dear reader, that I have never taken drugs) but could never put into words, certainly not in any scientific form. (If you're interested read my novel, *Tomy und der Planet der Lüge*).

In other words, maybe we don't need to resort to interstellar travel, use up our valuable raw materials, or build expensive radio telescopes, and we certainly don't have to send out waves of colonists into space. All the knowledge we could ever need is right at our fingertips—hidden somewhere in every electron. We simply need to find a way of getting to it.

Space Travel, to Be on the Safe Side

If we had access to the entire knowledge of the universe, we would be almost divine. If individual people ever achieve this level of insight—maybe old monks sitting in their cells—they would never be able to put it into words. There are no words for the unthinkable. We are all transitory beings: our intellects and our psyches demand material confirmation. Proof comes from seeing and touching. No message from a saint or announcement from a medium could ever be enough for us. Belief in something proclaimed by someone else is just not scientific. If we were to believe instead of know, we would have just the sort of chaos wreaked by religions the world over. It's no secret that every religion in our earthly madhouse maintains that it is the only one that preaches the genuine truth. Faith creates fear and insecurity. Nobody knows whether other people's proclamations are holy or just seem that way. Secretly we are all looking for perfection—but not via belief. Faith is an artificial construct—a "must" that doesn't satisfy curiosity. Knowledge demands facts.

In other words, despite the cosmic consciousness, despite the memes, and despite the hints of a grandiose infinitude, we will continue to search for proof. These proofs have to be material, accessible, and visible to satisfy those who are uncertain. Every doubt wants reality. This level of certainty will not arise until we have our first contact with an extraterrestrial civilization. Hurrah! That's happened already!

Among the possibilities for interstellar encounters we've mentioned so far, the only thing that's missing is a "von Neumann machine." What's one of those? A von Neumann machine is a technical device capable of self-replication. Humanity sends a von Neumann machine out into the next solar system. Once there, it seeks out suitable planets and starts to produce copies of itself. Then two von Neumann machines start out, then four, then eight, and so on. It creates a kind of snowball effect, and within a calculable time frame—depending on velocities involved—our whole galaxy would be "infected" with von Neumann machines. These wouldn't need to be huge devices. A device the size of a macro-molecule riding on the tip of a laser beam would be enough.

Extraterrestrials? Contact with them? One of today's most brilliant forward thinkers in this respect is Professor Michio Kaku, a physicist at City University in New York. Following a lecture in Switzerland, Kaku was interviewed by the astronomer Dr. Stefan Thiessen. He wanted to know how we should understand the term cosmic evolution. According to Kaku:

> When the time comes for us to head off into space, we will have nanotechnology at our disposal which will help us cope with the rough conditions of the extreme reaches of outer space. If we actually do meet up with some other civilization out there in space, then these beings might be part organic, part computer. Even the starships themselves could be living organisms. Professor Freemann Dyson wrote about "Astrochickens," a kind of genetically enhanced intelligent starship which uses "chicken technology" to replicate itself [*i.e., lay "eggs"*; author's addition/ emphasis].[28]

Professor Kaku subdivides extraterrestrial civilizations into various types or categories. We belong to type 0, which is the most primitive of all of the galactic families. Type I is already advanced enough to have stopped warring and is capable of deploying resources globally. Type II is a space-traveling civilization, uses unimaginable energies directly from the hearts of stars, and is already colonizing the galaxy. Type III civilizations are, from our human perspective, "godlike." They can do pretty much what they want to where they want to. Alluding to the Fermi paradox, Dr. Thiessen asked whether type III civilizations would even be interested in communicating with less developed species. Professor Kaku's opinion is: "Well, I would assume that they would be interested and therefore want to make contact with other civilizations. Having said that, for a type III civilization we would be little more than ants so the level of contact would be rather limited."[29]

During the conversation, Professor Kaku also claimed that type III civilizations could have sent spies out into the universe—in other words, small units that would send back word when they discovered other civilizations. Making full use of nanotechnology, these spies could be "no bigger than a bread basket" or even smaller.

It's even possible that extraterrestrial spies have already been watching us for thousands of years—and we simply do not recognize them. A spy could be a stone, a computer, or even a person. We all carry information about the past right up to the present within us. The electrons ensure that the message is passed on, even out into the universe.

Judgment Day

Our current knowledge about cosmic physics is still in its infancy. Astrophysicists have measured the amount of "dark matter" in space and discovered that there is five times as much dark matter as normal matter—but nobody knows what it is. They have the same problem with "dark energy": It seems to be completely immaterial and yet contains around three times as much energy as the ominous dark matter. A massive 77 percent of the universe consists of dark matter, so is it any great surprise that, faced with these invisible and yet measurable dimensions, astrophysicists start thinking about parallel worlds—

worlds that exist alongside ours and whose existence we barely suspect, at best? Maybe some invisible brother is looking over my shoulder right now and—again maybe—supplying me with information.

One thing is certain: At some stage, we *will* have contact with an extraterrestrial life form. This meeting will be "Judgment Day" for the world's religions. All religions are basically intolerant, even when many of their followers claim to be otherwise. Despite all the talk of conciliation and all the alleged understanding for those of other faiths, at the end of the day the most important thing that remains is each religion's claim that *only it* professes the absolute truth. If this truth disappears in a puff of smoke, then what remains for the religions? Christians cannot suddenly claim that the word of Jesus in the gospels is false. After all, it's all supposed to come directly from the son of God. In just the same way, Muslims cannot turn around and say that the texts in the Holy Qur'an did not originate with the founder of their religion. Added to this, the followers of the Jewish world religion claim to be the "chosen ones"; and for Muslims, anyone who believes differently is an "infidel." Ultimately, the believers of all three major semitic religions—Christianity, Judaism, and Islam—think they are in sole possession of the absolute truth. They must all dread the day when we finally encounter extraterrestrials. Is this perhaps a hidden reason for a certain tendency among them to exhibit no small degree of animosity toward science? A religion that ignores scientific findings and keeps scientific evidence from its followers is dogmatic. In other words, conflict with the ETs is inevitable. Religious cantankerousness and the superior knowledge of the extraterrestrials are hardly an ideal mix.

"What if it were the other way round?" ask well-meaning critics. What if we humans really are numero uno in the universe? If we really are the first intelligent life form? If all the projects that I've outlined here—from the von Neumann machines and the warp drive to panspermia—originated solely with us? Sometime in the next couple of centuries, perhaps.

This way of thinking would be all right but for the fact the ETs have already visited the Earth at least one time already. I *know* the names and trades of some of the aliens that communicated with selected humans many thousands of years ago. How do I know that? Did I have some kind of epiphany? Did some spirit whisper them into my ears, or was I infected by some kind of memes?

Nonsense! Anyone who wants to know the names of the ETs can read them in the Book of Enoch. (I wrote extensively about Enoch in my last book, *History Is Wrong.*) So what do we do with this knowledge? Nothing.

Knowledge for the Hens!

Everyone knows the famous stone circle Stonehenge in the south of England. What's that got to do with extraterrestrials?

By the order of his monarch, King Charles I (1600–1649), court architect and surveyor Inigo Jones (1573–1652) did an extensive survey of Stonehenge, looking closely at the ancient records. He found out that the stone circle was erected to honor the god Coelus. In his report to the king, Jones wrote:

> I conceive it not be impertinent to our purpose in hand to deliver what the Ancients have reported of Cœlus...he which first reigned over the Atlantide was Cœlus...he invited men living dispersedly throughout the fields to convene and dwell in companies together, exhorting them to build towns and reducing them from wild and savage is to the conversation of civil life: ...Taught them also how to sow corn and seeds.... He was a diligent observer of the stars and foretold men divers things to come...according to the course of the Sun [he divided the year] into months.... Whereby many ignorant of the perpetual course of the stars and amazed at his future predictions did verily believe that he participate of divine nature...they conferred on him imortal honours and adored him as a God. And, as he appeared, called him Cœlus in regard of his skill in the celestial bodies...all of these stones erected in antiquity

are like symbolic flames with which the heavens were honoured...
in this antiquity many stones were put together in imitation of a
constellation of stars which appear to us in the sky in the form
of a circle called the heavenly crown...it is not improbable that
Stonehenge was so composed because it was dedicated to this God
Cœlus....[30]

Was information like this ever taken seriously by anybody? Just
one hundred years ago, academics compared this culture bringer who
descended from the heavens with some kind of "anthropomorphized
natural elemental."[31] The perception of sun and moon played a decisive
role in the confused heads of our forefathers, I read. Undoubtedly(!),
the beings who taught the skills of crops and tools had a "lunar nature"
as they just as quickly "waxed, waned or fragmented" just like the phases
of the moon. With this way of looking at things it's no wonder that
beard and head hairs become "rays of sun" and the heavenly teachers
become stars, which admittedly also can appear and then disappear.

These quotes are hundreds of years old, but little has changed. We
still cling to the dated templates from the psychologists, and in the
process consider ourselves to be well-educated. I admit that I have a
certain degree of respect for the interpretations of earlier centuries.
Today is it really still necessary to keep on peddling this nonsense as
"scientific" to students and the faithful of the many different religions?
And from which "divine mouths" are the precise information about
the calendars, the leap years, and the names of the extraterrestrials
supposed to have come from in these psychologically motivated
notions? Those that were written down thousands of years ago.

Puma Punku, which I talked about in Chapter 1, is the real McCoy!
It's verifiable! For that reason alone, we should stop letting the
establishment lead us around by the nose. Maybe then we'll be in a
better position to cope with the return of the gods.

Notes

Chapter 1

1. Pauwels and Bergier, Aufbruch.
2. *Ibid.*
3. Ibid.
4. Kiss, *Das Sonnentor.*
5. Ibid.
6. Pauwels and Bergier, *Aufbruch.*
7. All Bible quotations, unless otherwise noted, come from *Die Heilige.*
8. Berdyczewski, *Die Sagen.*
9. Kautzsch, *Die Apokryphen.*
10. Apollonius, *Die Argonauten.*
11. See Mooney, *The Argonautica*; Delage and Vian, *Apollonius*; Radermacher, *Mythos*; and Meuli, *Odyssee.*
12. Burckhardt, *Gilgamesch.*
13. Kramer, *Geschichte.*
14. See Schultze-Jena, *Popol Vuh* and Cordan, *Popol Vuh: das Buch des Rates Schöpfungsmythos und Wanderung der Quiché-Maya.*
15. Freuchen, *Peter.*
16. Bezold, *Kebra Nagast.*
17. Kautzsch, *Die Apokryphen.*
18. Weidenreich, *Apes.*
19. Saurat and Streller, *Atlantis.*
20. Dougherty, *Valley.*
21. Glaubrecht, "Saurier."
22. Ibid.
23. Stiegner, *Die Königin.*

24. Cremo and Thompson, *Verbotene.*

25. Hartmann et al, *Origin.*

26. Kleine et al, "Hf-W Chronometry. "

27. If you read the "scientific" literature, you'll usually find that the age of the moon is given at around 4.5 billion years. I'm not entirely convinced, but that's a story for another day.

28. Davies, *Der kosmische.*

29. Gardner, "Bio-Kosmosos."

30. Däniken, *Der Götter-Schock* (page 186 ff.) and Däniken, *Die Götter waren* (page 77 ff.).

31. Blackmore, *Die Macht.*

32. Cieza de Leon, *La crónica.*

33. De la Vega, *Primera.*

34. Betanzos, *Suma.*

35. Moline, *Relación.*

36. Castro y del Castillo, *Teatro.*

37. Balboa, *Histoire.*

38. Alcino, *Die Kunst.*

39. d'Orbigny, *Voyage.*

40. Tschudi, *Reisen.*

41. Stübel and Uhle, *Die Ruinenstätte.*

42. Ibid.

43. Ibid.

44. Ibid.

45. Middendorf, *Das Runa* and Middendorf, *Wörterbuch.*

46. Tschudi, *Reisen.*

47. Posnansky, *Tihuanacu.*

48. Posnansky, *Eine falsche.*

49. Posnansky, *Tihuanacu.*

50. Ibid.

51. Ibid.

52. Ibid.

53. Ibid.

54. Ibid.

55. Ibid.

56. Ibid.

57. Kiss, *Das Sonnentor.*

58. Ibid.

59. Ibid.

60. Ibid.

61. Bellamy and Allan, *The Great.*

62. Apelt, *Platon.*

63. Tschudi, *Reisen.*

64. Luizaga, *Das Sonnentor.*

65. See Manzanilla, *Akapana*; Escalante Moscoso, *Arquitectura*; and Sanginés, *Tiwanaku.*

66. Protzen and Nair, "On Reconstructing."

67. Ibid.

68. Däniken, *History.*

69. Hausdorf, "Neue Rätsel."

Chapter 2

1. Schweitzer, "Dubiose."

2. Ibid.

3. Kulke, "Auferstehung."

4. The original German title of the book was *Erinnerungen an die Zukunft,* which translates as "Memories of the Future." Book titles of translated books, however, are usually thought up by the publishers in each country where the book is published and often the original sense is lost entirely for the sake of attracting readers' attention with a snappy title.

5. Däniken, *Erinnerungen.*

6. Unger, *Chronologie.*

7. Wadell, *Manetho.*

8. Karst, *Eusebius.*

9. See Chapter 2 of my book *History Is Wrong.*

10. See page 243 of *Tayos Gold* (German version) by Stan Hall.

11. Däniken, *History.*

12. Eberhard, *Beiträge.*

13. Herodotus, *Historien.*

14. Mariette, *Le Séraphéum.*

15. Herodotus, *Historien.*

16. Mariette, *Le Séraphéum.*

17. Ibid.

18. Mond, *The Bucheum.*

19. Ibid.

20. Mariette, *Le Séraphéum.*

21. Leca, *Die Mumien.*

22. Karst, *Eusebius.*

Chapter 3

1. Christenson, *Popol Vul.*

2. Faulkner, *The Ancient.*

3. Feyerabend, *Naturphilosophie.*

4. Brugsch, *Die Sage.*

5. Ibid.

6. Ibid.

7. Lurker, *Lexikon.*

8. This and the following Bible quotes come from *Die Heilige Schrift des Alten und des Neuen Testamente.*

9. Däniken, *Prophet.*

10. Cordan, *Popol Vuh—Das Buch des Rates. Mythos und Geschichte der Maya.*

11. Christenson, *Popol Vuh.*

12. Ibid.

13. Ebermann, *Sagen.*

14. Krehl, *Über die Religion.*

15. Herodotus, *Historien.*

Chapter 4

1. Ceram, *Götter.*

2. Fagan, *Die Vergrabene.*

3. Vollemaere, *The Mayan.*

4. See Landa, *Relación,* and its translation: Landa, *Yucatan.*

5. Ibid.

6. Acosta, *Historia.*

7. Deckert, *Maya-Handschrift.*

8. Barthel, "Die Gegenwärtige."

9. Barthel, "Mayahieroglyphen."

10. Wilson, "Astronomical."

11. Förstermann, "Die Astronomie," and Förstermann, "Blatt."

12. Noll-Husum, "Grundlegendes."

13. Henseling, "Das Alter."

14. Webber, *The Thunderbird.*

15. Marriott and Rachlin, *Plains.*

16. Coffer, *Spirits.*

17. Ibid.

18. Teit, Gould, et al, *Folk-tales.*

19. Morriseau, *Legends.*

20. Ibid.

21. See Blumrich, *Kasskara,* and Waters, *Book.*

22. Däniken, *History.*

23. Worcester Makemson, *The Book.*

24. Ludwiger, *UFOs,* pp. 351 ff.

25. Ayoub, *Redemptive.*

26. Sachedina, *Islamic.*

27. Ibid.

28. Dalberg, *Scheik.*

29. See Widengren, *Hochgottglaube,* and Reitzenstein, *Das Iranische.*

30. All quotations in ts paragraphare from Abegg, Der Messiasglaube.

31. Roy, *The Mahabharata.*

32. Glasenapp, *Der Jainismus.*

33. Schomerus, *Indische.*

34. Diodorus of Sicily, *Geschichts-Bibliothek.*

35. Riessler, *Altjüdisches.*

36. Burrows, *Mehr Klarheit.*

37. Kautzsch, *Die Apokryphen.*

38. Bonwetsch, *Das Sogenannte.*

39. Grömling, *Tibets.*

40. Grünwedel, *Mythologie.*

41. Gressmann, *Der Messias.*

42. Grömling, *Tibets.*

43. The entire text of the Book of Mormon can be found online at*scriptures.lds.org/bm/contents.*

44. Unger, *Chronologie.*

45. Karst,*Eusebius.*

46. Herodotus, *Historien.*

47. Diodorus of Sicily, *Geschichts-Bibliothek.*

48. Ruzo, *La Historia.*

49. Eissmann, *El Enladrillado.*

50. Ibid.

Chapter 5

1. Kant, *Kritik.*

2. Crawford, *"Where."*

3. Hosek, *"Economics."*

4. Swenson, *" Intergalactically."*

5. Ibid.

6. Haviland, *"Requirements."*

7. Ibid.

8. Obousy, *"Creating."*

9. Long, *"A Theoretical."*

10. Papagiannis, *"TheIimportance."*

11. Ibid.

12. Crawford, "Where."

13. Däniken, *Beweise,* Chapter 5.

14. Vollmert, *Das Molekül.*

15. Hoyle, *Das Intelligente.*

16. Hoyle and Wickramasinghe, *Evolution.*

17. Horn, *Götter gaben.*

18. Lossau, *"Auch Außerirdische."*

19. Chardin, *Der Mensch.*

20. Valiante, *"Der «Außerirdische»."*

21. Ambjørn and Loll, *"The Self-Organizing."*

22. Charon, *Der Geist.*

23. Charon, *La Théorie.*

24. Charon, Der Geist.

25. Sudhoff, *Ewiges.*

26. Ibid.

27. Ibid.

28. Thiessen and Kaku, "Lebendige."

29. Ibid.

30. Jones, *The Most.*

31. All of the quotations in this paragraph are from Ehrenreich, *"Die Mythen."*

BIBLIOGRAPHY

Abegg, Emil. *Der Messiasglaube in Indien und Iran.* Berlin/Leipzig, Germany: W. de Gruyter, 1928.

Acosta, José de. *Historia Natural y Moral de los Indias. Volume VI.* Seville, Spain: Juan de Leon, 1590.

Alcino, José. *Die Kunst des alten Amerika.* Freiburg, Germany: Herder Verlag, 1979.

Ambjørn, Jan, Jerzy Jurkiewicz, and Renate Loll. "The Self-Organizing Quantum Universe." *Scientific American,* July 2008.

Apelt, Otto. *Platon—Sämtliche Dialoge. Volume VII, Gesetze.* Hamburg, Germany: Meiner, 1988.

Apollonius of Rhodes. *Die Argonauten des Apollonius.* Zürich, Switzerland: Drell, Geßner, Füßlin und Compagnie, 1779.

Ayoub, Mahmoud. *Redemptive Suffering in Islam.* New York/Paris: Mouton De Gruyter, 1978.

Balboa, Miguel Cabello de. *Histoire de Pérou.* Translated by H. Ternaux-Compans. Paris: Arthus Bertrands, 1840.

Barthel, Thomas. "Die Gegenwärtige Situation in der Erforschung der Maya-Schrift" in "Proceedings of the Thirty-Second International Congress of Americanists, Copenhagen, 8–14 August 1956." Copenhagen, Denmark: Munksgaard, 1958.

——. "Mayahieroglyphen." *Bild der Wissenschaft, issue 6,* June 1967. Munich, Germany: Deutsche Verlags-Anstalt, 2000.

Bellamy, Hans Schindler, and Peter Allan. *The Great Idol of Tiahuanaco.* London: Faber and Faber, 1959.

Berdyczewski, Micha Josef (Bin Gorion). *Die Sagen der Juden. Volume III, Juda und Israel.* Frankfurt am Main, Germany: Rütten & Loening, 1927.

——. *Die Sagen der Juden von der Urzeit.* Frankfurt am Main, Germany: Rütten & Loening, 1913.

Betanzos, Juan de. *Suma y narración de los Incas.* Madrid, Spain: Manuel G. Hernández, 1880.

Bezold, Carl. Kebra Nagast. *Die Herrlichkeit der Könige.* Munich, Germany: Akademie der Wissenschaften, 1905.

Blackmore, Susan. *Die Macht der Meme.* Heidelberg, Germany: Spektrum Akademischer Verlag, 2000.

Blumrich, Josef F. *Kasskara und die sieben Welten.* Düsseldorf, Germany: Econ, 1979.

Bonwetsch, Gottlieb Nathanael. *Das sogenannte slawische Henochbuch.* Leipzig, Germany: J.C. Hinrichs, 1922.

The Book of Mormon. The Official Scriptures of The Church of Jesus Christ of Latter-day Saints. *scriptures.lds.org/bm/contents.* Copyright 2010, Intellectual Reserve, Inc.

Brugsch, Heinrich. *Die Sage von der geflügelten Sonnenscheibe nach altägyptischen Quellen.* Göttingen: Dieterich, Germany, 1870.

Burckhardt, Georg. *Gilgamesch, eine Erzählung aus dem alten Orient.* Wiesbaden, Germany: Insel-Verlag, 1958.

Burrows, Millar. *Mehr Klarheit über die Schriftrollen.* Munich, Germany: Beck, 1958.

Castro y del Castillo, Antonio de. *Teatro Eclesiástico de las Iglesias del Perú y Nueva España.* Madrid, Spain: D. Gil González Dávila, 1651.

Ceram, C.W. *Götter, Gräber und Gelehrte.* Hamburg, Germany: Rowohlt, 1949.

Chardin, Pierre Teilhard de. *Der Mensch im Kosmos.* Munich, Germany: C.H. Beck, 1965.

Charon, Jean E. *Der Geist der Materie.* Hamburg, Germany: Zsolnay-Verlag, 1979.

——. *La Théorie de la Relativité Complexe.* Paris : A. Michel, 1977.

Christenson, Allen. *Popol Vuh, Vol. II Literal Poetic Version.* Norman, Okla.: University of Oklahoma Press, 2004.

Cieza de Leon, Pedro. *Parte Primera de la Crónica del Perú.* Sevilla, Spain: Por Martín de Montesdoca, 1553.

——. *Segunda Parte de la Crónica del Perú.* Madrid, Spain: Marcos Jiménez de la Espada, 1880.

Coffer, William E. (Koi Hosh). *Spirits of the sacred mountains—Creation stories of the American Indian.* New York: Van Nostrand Reinhold Co., 1978.

Cordan, Wolfgang. *Popol Vuh—Das Buch des Rates. Mythos und Geschichte der Maya.* Düsseldorf, Germany: Eugen Diederichs Verlag, 1962.

———. *Popol Vuh: das Buch des Rates Schöpfungsmythos und Wanderung der Quiché-Maya.* Düsseldorf, Germany: Eugen Diederichs Verlag, 1962.

Crawford, Ian. "Where Are They?" *Scientific American,* July 2000.

Cremo, Michael A., and Richard L. Thompson. *Verbotene Archäologie.* Rottenburg, Germany: Kopp, 2008.

d'Orbigny, Alcide. *Voyage dans l'Amérique Méridionale.* Paris : Bertrand, 1844.

Dalberg, Johann Friedrich von. *Scheik Mohammed Fani's Dabistan oder von der Religion der ältesten Parsen.* Aschaffenburg, Germany: Erlinger, 1809.

Däniken, Erich von. *Beweise.* Düsseldorf, Germany: Econ, 1977.

———. *Der Götter-Schock.* Munich, Germany: Bertelsmann, 1992.

———. *Der Tag, an dem die Götter kamen.* Munich, Germany: Bertelsmann, 1984.

———. *Die Götter waren Astronauten.* Munich, Germany: Bertelsmann, 2001.

———. *Erinnerungen an die Zukunft.* Düsseldorf, Germany: Econ Verlag, 1968.

———. *History Is Wrong.* Franklin Lakes, N.J.: Career Press, 2009.

———. *Prophet der Vergangenheit.* Düsseldorf, Germany: Econ, 1979.

———. *Tomy und der Planet der Lüge.* A novel. Rottenburg: Kopp, 2007.

Davies, Paul. *Der Kosmische Volltreffer.* Frankfurt am Main, Germany: Campus Verlag GmbH, 2008.

De la Vega, Garcilaso. *Historia General del Perú.* Madrid, Spain: Madrid Oficina Real, 1722.

———. *Primera Parte de los Comentarios Reales.* Madrid, Spain: Nicolas Rodriguez Franco, 1723.

Deckert, Helmut. *Maya-Handschrift der Sächsischen Landesbibliothek Dresden. Codex Dresdensis.* Berlin: Akademie-Verlag, 1962.

Delage, Emile, and Francis Vian. *Apollonius de Rhodes: Argonautique. Tome III, Chant IV.* Paris: Les Belles Lettres, 1981.

Die Heilige Schrift des Alten und des Neuen Testamentes. Stuttgart, Germany: Württembergische Bibelanstalt, 1972.

Diodorus of Sicily. *Geschichts-Bibliothek, 2. Buch.* Translated by Dr. Adolf Wahrmund. Stuttgart, Germany: Hoffmann'sche Verlags-Buchhandlung, 1867.

Dougherty, Cecil N. *Valley of Giants, the Latest Discoveries in Palaeontology.* Cleburne, Tex.: Bennet Publishing Company, 1971.

Eberhard, Otto. *Beiträge zur Geschichte des Stierkultes in Ägypten.* Leipzig, Germany: G. Olms, 1938.

Ebermann, Oskar. *Sagen der Technik.* Leipzig, Germany: Hegel & Schade, 1930.

Ehrenreich, Paul. "Die Mythen und Legenden der südamerikanischen Urvölker und ihre Beziehungen zu denen Nordamerikas und der Alten Welt." *Zeitschrift für Ethnologie,* Wiegandt & Hempel, 1905.

Eissmann, Rafael Videla. *El Enladrillado, una Meseta Prediluvial en los Andes.* Santiago, Chile: Tierra Polar, 2008.

Escalante Moscoso, Javier F. *Arquitectura prehispánica en los Andes Bolivianos.* La Paz, Bolivia: Producciones CIMA, 1994.

Fagan, Brian M. *Die Vergrabene Sonne.* Munich, Germany: Piper Verlag GmbH, 1979.

Faulkner, Raymond Oliver. *The Ancient Egyptian Pyramid Texts.* Oxford, UK: Aris & Phillips, 1969.

Feyerabend, Paul. *Naturphilosophie.* Frankfurt am Main, Germany: Suhrkamp, 2009.

Förstermann, Erns. "Blatt Sechzig der Dresdner Maya-Handschrift." *Das Weltall, sixth year, issue 16* May 15, 1906.

——. "Die Astronomie der Mayas. " *Das Weltall, fourth year, issue 19,* July 1, 1904.

Freuchen, Peter. *Peter Freuchen's Book of the Eskimos.* Greenwich, UK: Arthur Barker, 1961.

Gardner, James N. "Bio-Kosmos, Intelligentes Leben als Architekt des Universums? " Lecture at the WORLD MYSTERIES FORUM, May 11, 2008, Basel, Switzerland.

——. "Virtual interstellar Cloning." Presentation at the IAA Symposium, September 22–26, 2008, Paris.

Glasenapp, Helmuth von. *Der Jainismus. Eine indische Erlösungsreligion.* Berlin: A. Häger, 1925.

Glaubrecht, Matthias. "Saurier und Primaten lebten Seite an Seite." *DIE WELT, June 14, 2004,* page 35.

Gressmann, Hugo. *Der Messias.* Göttingen, Germany: Vandenhoeck & Ruprecht, 1929.

Grömling, Willi. *Tibets altes Geheimnis—Gesar, ein Sohn des Himmels.* Gross-Gerau, Germany: Ancient Mail, 2005.

Grünwedel, Albert. *Mythologie des Buddhismus in Tibet und in der Mongolei.* Leipzig, Germany: Brockhaus, 1900.

Hartmann, William K., et al. *Origin of the Moon.* Houston, Texas: Lunar & Planetary Institute, 1986.

Hausdorf, Hartwig. "Neue Rätsel im Hochland der Anden." *Brisante Archäologie.* Edited by Erich von Däniken.Rottenburg, Germany: Kopp, 2008.

Haviland, Robert P. "Requirements for Interstellar Travel." *Journal of the British Interplanetary Society, 60,* 2007.

Henseling, Robert. "Das Alter der Maya-Astronomie und die Oktaeteris." *Nachrichtenblatt der deutschen Wissenschaft und Technik, 25th year, issue 3/4.*

Herodotus. *Historien, griechisch–deutsch. Volume II.* Munich, Germany: Ernst Heimeran Verlag, 1963.

Horn, Arthur David. *Götter Gaben uns die Gene.* Berlin: Silberschnur, 1997.

Hosek, William. "Economics and the Fermi Paradox." *Journal of the British Interplanetary Society, 60: 137–41,* 2007.

Hoyle, Fred. *Das intelligente Universum.* Frankfurt am Main, Germany: Umschau-Verlag, 1984.

Hoyle, Fred, and Nalin Chandra Wickramasinghe. *Evolution aus dem All*. Frankfurt am Main, Germany: Ullstein, 1981.

Jones, Inigo. *The Most Notable Antiquity of Great Britain Vulgarly Called Stonehenge*. 1655. Reprinted in London by Scolar Press in 1973.

Kant, Immannuel. *Kritik der reinen Vernünft*. Leipzig, Germany: Reclam, 1787.

Karst, Josef. "Eusebius Werke." *Die Chronik, Volume 5*, 1911.

Kautzsch, Emil. *Die Apokryphen und Pseudepigraphen des Alten Testamentes. 2 volumes: Das Buch Baruch*. Tübingen, Germany: J.C.B. Mohr (Paul Siebeck), 1900.

——. *Die Apokryphen und Pseudepigraphen des Alten Testamentes. 2 volumes: Das Buch Henoch*. Tübingen, Germany: J.C.B. Mohr (Paul Siebeck), 1900.

Kiss, Edmund. *Das Sonnentor von Tihuanaku und Hörbigers Welteislehre*. Leipzig, Germany: Koehler & Amelang, 1937.

Kleine, Thorsten, et al. "Hf-W Chronometry of Lunar Metals and the Age and Early Differentiation of the Moon." *SCIENCE, Vol. 310:1671–4*, December 9, 2005.

Kramer, Samual Noah. *Geschichte beginnt mit Sumer*. Wiesbaden, Germany: List, 1959.

Krannich, Paul Heiner. "Die Pharaonen des Manethos." *Sagenhafte Zeiten, seventh year, No. 4*, 2005.

Krehl, Ludolf. *Über die Religion der vorislamischen Araber*. Leipzig, Germany: Serig'sche, 1863.

Kulke, Ulli. "Auferstehung der Toten." *DIE WELT,* May 23, 2008.

Landa, Diego de. *Relación de las Cosas de Yucatán*. 1566. (Handwritten manuscript discovered in the Biblioteca de la Real Academia de Historia de Madrid in 1862.)

——. *Yucatan Before and After the Conquest*. New York: Courier Dover Publications, 1978. (A translation of Landa's *Relación de las Cosas de Yucatán* by William Gates.)

Las Ultimas Noticias (daily newspaper), October 26, 1968. Santiago, Chile.

Leca, Ange-Pierre. *Die Mumien: Zeugen ägyptischer Vergangenheit.* Düsseldorf: Econ, 1982.

Long, Kelvin. "A Theoretical Proposal for Interstellar Travel: Warp Drive." *Spaceflight Magazine, Vol. 50,* April 2008.

Lossau, Norbert. "Auch Außerirdische sind Gottes Geschöpfe." *DIE WELT,* May 15, 2008.

Lovelock, James. *Unsere Erde Wird überleben: Gaia, eine Optimische Ökologie.* Munich, Germany: Piper Verlag GmbH, 1982.

Ludwiger, Illobrand von. *UFOs, die Unerwünschte Wahrheit.* Rottenburg: Kopp, 2009.

Luizaga, Jorge Miranda. *Das Sonnentor.* Munich, Germany: Dianus-Trikont, 1985.

Lurker, Manfred. *Lexikon der Götter und Symbole der alten Ägypter.* Munich, Germany: O.W. Barth, 1974.

Manzanilla, Linda. *Akapana: Una Pirámide en el Centro del Mundo.* Instituto de Investigaciones Antropológicas, Mexico: Universidad Nacional Autónoma de México, 1992.

Mariette, Auguste. *Le Séraphéum de Memphis.* Paris: 1857. (Published by Gaston Maspero in 1882.)

Marriott, Alice, and Carol K. Rachlin. *Plains Indian Mythology.* New York: Crowell, 1975.

Meuli, Karl. *Odyssee und Argonautika. Untersuchungen zur Griechischen Sagengeschichte.* Berlin: Weidmann, 1921.

Middendorf, E.W. *Das Runa Simi oder die Keshua-Sprache.* Leipzig, Germany: F.A. Brockhaus, 1890.

——. *Wörterbuch des Runa Simi oder der Keshua-Sprache.* Leipzig, Germany: F.A. Brockhaus, 1890.

Moline, Cristóbal. *Relación de las Fábulas y Ritos de los Incas.* Lima, Peru: Sanmartí y ca., 1916.

Mond, Sir Robert. *The Bucheum. Volume I.* London: The Egypt Exploration Society, 1934.

Mooney, George W. *The Argonautica of Apollonius Rhodius.* Dublin, Ireland: Dublin University Press, 1912.

Morriseau, Norval. *Legends of My People, the Great Ojibway.* New York/London: Ryerson Press, 1965.

Noll-Husum, Herbert. "Grundlegendes zur Zeitbestimmung der Maya." *Zeitschrift für Ethnologie, 69th year, issue 1/3,* 1938.

Obousy, Richard. "Creating the 'Warp' in Warp Drives." *Spaceflight Magazine, Vol. 50,* April 2008.

Papagiannis, Michael. "The Importance of Exploring the Asteroid Belt." *Acta Astronautica, Volume 10: 709–12,.* Oxford: Pergamon Press, 1983.

Pauwels, Luis, and Jacques Bergier. *Aufbruch ins Dritte Jahrtausend.* Bern und Stuttgart, Germany: Scherz, 1962.

Posnansky, Arthur. *Eine Falsche Kritik Max Uhles.* Berlin: Unger, 1913.

——. *Tihuanacu: The Cradle of American Man Vols. I–II.* Translated into English by James F. Sheaver. New York: J.J. Augustin, 1945.

——. *Tihuanacu: The Cradle of American Man Vols. III–IV.* La Paz, Bolivia: Minister of Education, 1957.

Protzen, Jean-Pierre, and Stella Nair. "On Reconstructing Tiwanaku Architecture." *Journal of the Society of Architectural Historians, Vol 59, No. 3,* September 2000.

Radermacher, Ludwig. *Mythos und Sage bei den Griechen.* Munich, Germany: Rohrer, 1938.

Reitzenstein, Richard. *Das iranische Erlösungsmysterium: Religionsgeschichtliche Untersuchungen.* Bonn, Germany: A. Marcus & E. Weber, 1921.

Riessler, Paul. *Altjüdisches Schrifttum außerhalb der Bibel. Die Apokalypse des Abraham.* Augsburg, Germany: B. Filser Verlag, 1928.

Roy, Pratap Chandra. *The Mahabharata, Drona Parva.* Calcutta, India: Bhārata Press, 1888.

Ruzo, Daniel. *La Historia Fantástica de un Descubrimiento: Los Templos de Piedra de una Humanidad Desaparecida.* Mexico City, Mexico: Editorial Diana, 1974.

Sachedina, Abdulaziz Abdulhussein. *Islamic Messianism: The Idea of the Mahdi in Twelver Shi'ism.* New York: State University of New York Press, 1981.

Sanginés, Carlos P. *Tiwanaku—200 Años de Investigaciones Arqueológicas.* La Paz, Bolivia: Producciones CIMA, 1995.

Saurat, Denis, and Justus Streller. *Atlantis und die Herrschaft der Riesen.* Stuttgart, Germany: Günther, 1955.

Schomerus, Hilko Wiardo. *Indische und Christliche Enderwartungen und Erlösungshoffnung.* Gütersloh, Germany: Bertelsmann, 1941.

Schultze-Jena, Leonhard. *Popol Vuh, das Buch der Quiché Indianer von Guatemala.* Stuttgart, Germany: Gerdt Kutsche, 1944.

Schweitzer, Sandra. "Dubiose Mischung." *DIE WELT AM SONNTAG,* May 25, 2008.

Stan Hall. *Tayos Gold.* Rottenburg, Germany: Kopp, 2008.

Stiegner, Roswitha Germana. "Die Königin von Sabá in ihrem Namen." Doctoral thesis, dbv Verlag für die Technische Universität, Graz, Austria, 1979.

Stübel, Alfons, and Max Uhle. *Die Ruinenstätte von Tiahuanaco im Hochland des alten Peru.* Leipzig, Germany: K.W. Hiersemann, 1892.

Sudhoff, Heinke. *Ewiges Bewusstsein.* Munich, Germany: Universitas, 2005.

Swenson, Jr., George. "Intergalactically Speaking." *Scientific American,* July 2002.

Teit, James Alexander, Marian K. Gould, et al. *Folk-tales of Salishan and Sahaptin Tribes.* New York: American folk-lore society, 1917.

Thiessen, Stefan, and Michio Kaku. "Lebendige Raumschiffe und intelligente Saurier." *Brisante Archäologie,* 2008.

Tschudi, Johann Jakob von. *Reisen durch Südamerika.* Leipzig, Germany: F.A. Brockhaus, 1869.

Unger, Georg F. *Chronologie des Manetho.* Berlin: Weidmannsche Buchhandlung, 1867.

Vaas, R. "Fremde Intelligenzen—Rarität oder Regel?" *Bild der Wissenschaft, No. 2/2002,* 2002.

Valiante, Francesco M. "Der «Außerirdische» ist unser Bruder." *L'Osservatore Romano, No. 24,* June 13, 2008. (Original Italian in OR 5/14/2008: Osservatore Romano, Vatican.)

Vollemaere, Antoon Leon. *The Mayan Year of 365 Days in the Codices*. Mechelen, Belgium: Vlaams Instituut voor Amerikanistiek, 1973.

Vollmert, Bruno. *Das Molekül und das Leben.* Hamburg, Germany: Rowohlt, 1985.

Wadell, William Gillan. *Manetho*. Cambridge, Mass.: Harvard University Press, 1940.

Waters, Frank. *Book of the Hopi.* New York: Viking Press, 1971.

Webber, William L. *The Thunderbird "Tootooch" Legends: Folk Tales of the Indian Tribes of the Pacific Northwest Coast Indians.* Seattle, Wash.: Ace Printing Co., 1936.

Weidenreich, Franz. *Apes, Giants and Man.* Chicago, Ill.: The University of Chicago Press, 1946.

Widengren, Geo. *Hochgottglaube im Alten Iran: eine Religionsphänomenologische Untersuchung.* Uppsala/Leipzig, Germany: A.-b. Lundequistska bokhandeln, 1938.

Wilson, Robert W. "Astronomical Notes on the Maya Codices." *Papers of the Peabody Museum of American Archaeology and Ethnology, Harvard University, Vol. VI, No. 3,* 1924.

Worcester Makemson, Maud. *The Book of the Jaguar Priest. A Translation of the Book of Chilam-Balam of Tizimin with Commentary.* New York: Schuman, 1951.

Index

About the Author

ERICH VON DÄNIKEN was born on April 14, 1935, in Zofingen in Switzerland and attended the St. Michel Jesuit school in Fribourg. He published his first book, *Chariots of the Gods*, in 1968. It was a worldwide best-seller that has been followed by 31 further books. He is the most widely read and most copied nonfiction author in the world. His works have been translated into 28 different languages and have sold a total of 63 million copies. Several of his books have also been filmed, and Erich's ideas have been the inspiration for a whole range of different TV series.